# upside down cooking

# upside down cooking

**Dominic Franks**
@dominthekitchen

# Contents

06     **Introduction**

18     **Individual Tarts & Pies**

46     **Sharing is Caring**

78     **Special Occasions**

100    **Soups, Salads, & Sides**

122    **Right Side Up**

152    **Cakes & Desserts**

178    **Sweet Tarts of Joy**

202    **Index**

207    **Acknowledgments**

# Introduction

Welcome to *Upside Down Cooking*, the book that flips the art of cooking on its head, so you don't have to. In May 2023, inspired by the foodie world on social media and my love of everything wrapped in pastry, I created an upside-down caramelized onion tart, the video of which I posted on Instagram. There's nothing particularly incongruous about that and, to be honest, despite my usual predisposition for procrastination, I didn't think about it too deeply. I gave it my twist, adding a layer of luscious, salted cream cheese that lent a wonderful richness to the tart, filmed and uploaded it, then went to bed.

If I'm honest, I had become a little despondent with social media; it felt as though I was putting a lot of effort in for very little return, which had become frustrating and akin to shouting into the wind. I wanted to share my passion for cooking with the world, but not enough people were seeing my creations. Perhaps I was guilty of overthinking each image I posted instead of just getting on with it and sharing what I'd cooked that day.

However, with this little tart my life quite literally flipped upside down. I woke the next morning to a deluge of more than 6,000 comments, over 1.2 million likes, and 800,000 saves as well as close to 100,000 new followers. All in one day! The reel showing the tart has now been seen by more than 40 million people. With this simple tart, I tapped into viewers' and readers' desire for food that's delicious, looks great, and is not only easy but fun to make. And that is how *Upside Down Cooking* was born.

## A Bit About Me

For me, cooking is a generational thing with recipes passed down from parent to child and sideways across the family. This is how I grew up. Some of my earliest memories are sitting at one or the other of my grandmas' kitchen tables as she talked me through a recipe, where it came from, and how she cooked it. My mum still has a three-ring binder stuffed with handwritten recipes, some of them from my grandmas, some from aunts and great aunts, and all handed down with the reverence they deserve. Reading those recipes with Mum, learning their backstories and making them, is what inspired my love of cooking. I was so obsessed with wanting to cook that I sometimes pretended to be sick so I could stay home from school. The moment Mum went off to work, I would pull the binder down from the cupboard and start creating dishes. Mum always seemed impressed by the concoctions I presented her, although she wasn't happy about the mess left in her kitchen.

Food was central to everything our family did together. Our Jewish heritage meant that Friday night was the most important meal of the week, and Mum excelled at classic roast dinners with all the trimmings, although she would always put her 1970s or '80s spin on things—think mousses, roulades, and quiches as well as food set in gelatin. There was always a lot of gelatin!

Our larger family gatherings revolved around food too. Mum was famous for her buffet-style spreads: tables heaving with delicious treats, smoked salmon bagels, egg and onion salads, and fried fish balls. There would also be foods from farther afield, reflecting the melting pot of cultures in the area of London where we lived, including dishes such as curry, taramasalata, hummus, and tzatziki. Of course, now these dishes don't sound unusual, but when we were kids they offered new flavors that blew our sheltered suburban palates away, and we just loved it.

Once I'd left home to live on my own, I would often get creative in the kitchen for roommates and friends, not always successfully but my passion drove me to continue. I could always be relied on for a large pot of homemade soup, and I loved throwing a dinner party, designing a menu to suit the mood. Mum's homemade inspirations gave way to the other major cooking influence in my life, Delia Smith. Delia was one of the UK's first megastar TV cooks whose classic-but-simple recipes (and somewhat matronly attitude to cooking) allowed the nation to rise above our misguided reputation around the globe as a place of bad food and bad nutrition, and turned many of us into confident cooks. Her books, especially the *Complete Cookery Course* (which remains one of my most beloved and referred to cookbooks), were always reliable.

The advent of the internet, and specifically social media, allowed me a more immediate connection with people who shared my love of food. I started my recipe blog back in 2010 as a place to write down recipes and share them with like-minded foodies. It was a wonderfully diverse community of people, driven by a passion for food. I learned so much in those days, not just about cooking but also about writing and finding my style and tone of voice. The blog naturally transitioned to Instagram and the creation of short recipe videos or reels, which of course brings us full circle back to that infamous upside-down caramelized onion tart.

## What is Upside Down Cooking?

The upside-down idea is a simple one that encapsulates my style of cooking. You basically start with sugar or fat to help the cooking process, and then top these with the main ingredients. You're essentially building the recipe in reverse, creating a deconstructed version of a dish, and completing it with a blanket of pastry on top. Once in the oven, the heat from the metal sheet pan below and the cover of the pastry on top cooks the filling to glorious perfection, and then when it comes out of the oven you have the theatrics of flipping it over to reveal the finished dish.

And, of course, the possibilities are endless: from sweet to savory; and weekday meals to seasonal treats. Wherever your imagination and the ingredients in your fridge take you. I often ask guests who are coming to dinner what their favorite food is and then make it into an upside-down tart or pie, or take the essence of the dish and layer it under pastry. I love to take a classic recipe and think how it could work in layers. I ask myself "will it pie?" and if the answer is "yes" (which it almost inevitably is), then I adapt it to become an upside-down version. Once you have the technique figured out, you can get creative with your own inventions.

## About My Book

This book is packed with familiar dishes with an upside-down twist, alongside new creations inspired by my travels, meals out, family, and friends. There are chapters for individually sized savory tarts, pies, and canapés, all with a golden, crisp layer of puff pastry, pie crust, or phyllo dough. You'll also find recipes for large upside-down tarts and pies that are perfect for sharing and for special times of the year, such as Christmas, New Year's Eve, and Valentine's Day.

People often ask me what to serve with my upside-down tarts and pies, so there are recipes for soups, salads and sides that can be served alongside to make a complete meal, or extend it into a multiple-course dinner.

Alongside the upside-down recipes, I've included a chapter of some of my favorite right-side up dishes that follow the same principle of layering in terms of ingredients, textures, colors, and flavors to create well-rounded one-pot meals but without the flip.

And for those who love sweet treats (and who doesn't!), there is a collection of glorious cakes, baked goods, and tarts, all with my signature upside-down twist. Enjoy!

# Equipment & Ingredients

Simplicity is key when it comes to the way I like to cook, and that extends to the type of kitchen tools and ingredients I use. You're likely to have most of the equipment listed below, but I thought I'd share with you some of my most loved and used items, the stuff that works and brings me success. The same goes for basic ingredients; there is nothing fancy here, but they are all essentials when it comes to my style of upside-down cooking.

## Sheet pan

I use the Nordic Ware Jelly Roll Pan from their Naturals range, which measures 15 x 10½ in (38 x 27 cm). It's aluminum, which is a great conductor of heat, and has shallow sides, making it easier to slide a spatula under the tart, or for putting a cutting board on top for the flip. You don't want to be elbowing the sides of your sheet pan out the way and ruining the shape of the tart, but equally you don't want a flat sheet with the risk of the tart sliding off.

## Parchment paper

I would advise lining your sheet pan with parchment paper, also known as greaseproof paper or baking paper, because it prevents the tarts and pies from sticking to the pan and allows you to easily flip them over once baked. It also helps keep the fillings of the larger pies in place, and once flipped over will ensure you can peel off the paper to reveal the pie without damaging or losing the top. A small amount of butter around the inside edge of the pan also helps to hold the parchment paper in place.

## Egg wash

I always brush my pastry with a beaten egg before it goes into the oven. For an egg-free alternative, you can use a splash of milk or a milk alternative, or even a light vegetable oil. All give a beautifully bronzed pastry after baking.

## Food-safe pencil

For many of the recipes, I suggest tracing around a plate or a template with a pencil. It also helps

with knowing where to place the tart topping on the sheet pan if you mark the outline of the tart on the parchment paper first. You should use a food-safe pencil or, failing that, draw on one side of the paper and flip it over, since most parchment paper is opaque.

## Fats & sweeteners

Depending on which recipe you're making, the first ingredient used in all my tarts and pies, sweet or savory, is either a fat or sweetener. A drizzle of fat or sweetener over the parchment-paper-lined sheet pan helps cook and add color to your tart or pie, often creating a beautiful golden patina on the top and around the pastry edges. I use a good-quality extra-virgin olive oil (or sometimes butter) for the savory dishes. Honey is my preference for the sweet dishes, but this can be substituted for light corn syrup, maple syrup, or agave.

## Pastry

In the US, premade puff pastry and phyllo is fairly common and can be found in the freezer section of most supermarkets. Shortcrust or pie dough can also be found in the refrigerated section of most grocery stores in the US, with one problem—it's round! For many of these recipes, it might be easiest to make your own so you can roll it out to the desired size. Some supermarkets stock vegan and gluten-free versions of premade doughs, which are both perfectly good alternatives.

**Introduction**

## Pastry brush
This is a useful tool for brushing the egg wash over the pastry before baking to give it a golden glow. I prefer a silicone brush.

## Tape measure & templates
For ease and to avoid leftovers, the pastry sheets can be divided into evenly sized pieces with some simple math. A tape measure is handy for this, but I'd also suggest creating a cardboard template where directed in the recipe. You can also draw around a cake pan, ramekin, cookie cutter, or bowl for the circular tarts and pies.

Remember that pastry can stretch as you handle it, so don't worry if your tarts and pies come out a little wonky or misshapen; you can always trim the pastry once it's placed on the sheet pan.

### Tart & pie dimensions
Premade puff pastry comes in a variety of sizes and number of sheets per package. In this book, we encourage you to mark the dimensions for the tart in the recipe, then fit it to your sheet pan. You may have to use more than one. It's okay to get creative—and change the sizes if needed.

# My Go-To Pastry Recipes

If you can't get premade pastry easily or just want to make your own, here are two foolproof recipes that always work for me. One is a simple puff pastry, while the second is a classic pie dough. I've also included a few recipes for leftover pastry and my go-to sauces/condiments, which are used in many of the recipes in the book.

## Simple Puff Pastry
**MAKES ROUGHLY A 14 X 9 IN SHEET (500G)**

This recipe isn't quite as complicated or lengthy as making "real" puff pastry, but I think it tastes just as delicious and works well with my tarts and pies. Sure, it still takes a while because there are a few stages to master, but it delivers a wonderfully flaky, layered crust every time. It is inspired by my sister-in-law Mo's recipe, and she makes the best sausage rolls with it. It's definitely a lazy-day project. Put the kettle on, do a few jobs around the house, and come back to it every 20 minutes or so and by the end of the day, you'll have a stunning block of pastry ready to use as you wish.

2 cups (250g) all-purpose flour, plus extra for dusting
1 tsp fine sea salt
1 cup (250g) frozen salted butter, coarsely grated
roughly ⅔ cup (150ml) chilled water

1   Sift the flour and salt into a large bowl. Rub the butter loosely into the flour with your fingertips—you should be able to see flecks of butter. Make a well in the middle and pour in two-thirds of the chilled water, stirring with a clawed hand, until you have a rough dough. Add more water, if needed, to bring it together.

2   Flatten the dough out into a rough rectangle, wrap it in plastic wrap and leave to rest for 20 minutes in the freezer.

3   Turn the dough out onto a lightly floured worktop, knead gently, and form it into a smooth rectangle. Using a rolling pin, roll the dough in one direction, until three times the length, about 8 x 20 in (20 x 50 cm), with one of the short sides facing you. It should look marbled with butter.

4   Fold the top third down to the center and the bottom third up, like a letter. Give the dough a quarter turn to the right and roll it out again to three times the length, the same size as before. Fold as before. Wrap the pastry in plastic wrap and freeze for another 20 minutes before repeating this process twice more, turning the pastry a quarter turn to the right each time. The pastry is now ready to use or can be kept in the fridge for 3 days or the freezer for up to 3 months.

**Introduction**

## Classic Pie Dough
**MAKES ROUGHLY A 14 X 9 IN SHEET (400G)**

I learned to make pastry from Mum. When I was a kid, I used to spend hours propped up at the kitchen counter watching her make quiches and tarts, and they all started with a classic pie dough. Sure, she taught me about measurements and the ratio of fat to flour, but she also taught me not to worry about it all that much. Making pastry isn't science, it's just a combination of three simple, inexpensive ingredients. If you want to throw in ground almonds as well as flour or grated Cheddar cheese instead of some of the butter, then do it. Play with it ... what's the worst that can happen?

I loved watching Mum bring it all together in a bowl (or even in a food processor, which takes seconds), but most of all, of course, I loved what eventually came out of the oven. After all, anything wrapped in a gloriously golden, melt-in-the-mouth pastry must be good.

2 cups (250g) all-purpose flour
10 tbsp (150g) cold salted butter, diced
1–2 tbsp chilled water

**1** Sift the flour into a large bowl and rub in the butter with your fingertips until you have something resembling breadcrumbs. Keep your movements light and quick. Add a tablespoon or two of chilled water and bring it together into a ball of dough with your hands. You may need to add a little more water—the pastry should feel smooth and slightly dry, just damp enough to clean the inside of the bowl.

**2** Flatten the pastry slightly, wrap in plastic wrap and pop it in the fridge for at least 30 minutes before using. The pastry will keep in the fridge for up to 24 hours and can be frozen for up to 3 months.

**Note:** Pie dough can also be made in a food processor. Place the flour and butter in first and whiz to the breadcrumb stage, then add the water and whiz again until a smooth ball of dough forms.

# Leftover Pastry

I've tried to avoid any waste, but there will inevitably be a few off-cuts or leftover pastry with some of the recipes in this book. I think my main tip is that the freezer is your best friend. Pastry freezes well and lasts for up to 3 months if properly wrapped. Shape your leftover pastry into an evenly thick piece and wrap in plastic wrap. Place layers of wrapped pastry, with parchment paper between each one, in a freezer-proof bag, then store in the freezer. This way you can take as little or as much as you need each time. Here, are a few simple recipes to make use of any off-cuts you may want to use up.

## Pesto Cheese Twists or Pinwheels
**MAKES 8 TWISTS/PINWHEELS**

7oz (200g) leftover puff pastry off-cuts, defrosted if frozen
all-purpose flour, for dusting
3½oz (100g) Cheddar cheese, finely grated
1¾oz (50g) Parmesan cheese, finely grated
2 tbsp Pesto (see p.17), or use premade

**YOU WILL NEED**
large sheet pan, roughly 15 x 10½ in (38 x 27 cm), lined with parchment paper

1  Preheat the oven to 425°F (220°C).

2  Lightly knead your puff pastry off-cuts into a ball and then flatten out onto a lightly floured worktop with your hand. Using a rolling pin, roll the pastry into an 8-in (20-cm) square. Cut the pastry into 8 strips, roughly 1 in (2.5 cm) wide, and lay these on the lined sheet pan.

3  Mix together the Cheddar and Parmesan in a bowl. Spread a little pesto over each strip and then sprinkle with the cheese mix. These can then either be rolled up into pinwheels or twisted to make sticks. Bake for 15–20 minutes, until golden and puffy. Serve warm.

**Note:** These are such a fun, quick treat to make, and for a cheese-aholic like me they're dangerously addictive. You can get as adventurous with the flavorings as you like, adding your favorite toppings, such as yeast extract, ham slices, or chutney. For a sweet version, try chocolate spread or jam and sprinkle with chopped pistachios or your favorite nuts.

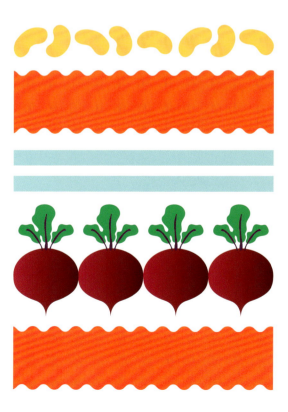

Introduction

## Cinnamon Puffs
**MAKES ROUGHLY 30 (A LARGE BOWLFUL)**

1 tbsp ground cinnamon
2 tbsp powdered sugar, sifted
7oz (200g) leftover puff pastry off-cuts, defrosted if frozen, and rolled out thinly
1 egg, beaten

**YOU WILL NEED**
large sheet pan, roughly 15 x 10½ in (38 x 27 cm), lined with parchment paper
large, sealable plastic bag

1  Preheat the oven to 425°F (220°C).

2  Put the cinnamon and sugar into the large plastic bag. Set aside.

3  Cut your rolled-out puff pastry off-cuts into bite-size chunks. They can be any size as long as they look as though they can be easily thrown into your mouth!

4  Spread out the pastry bites on the lined sheet pan and brush with egg. Bake for 10 minutes, or until golden and puffy. The moment they come out of the oven, carefully put the pastry puffs into the bag of cinnamon sugar. Seal the bag and shake until they are completely coated. Serve warm.

**Note:** A big batch of these simple sugar- and cinnamon-spiced puffs could replace a bowl of popcorn for your next movie night. They're ridiculously easy, quick, and tasty!

## Monkey Pie Crust
**PERFECT FOR THE TOP OF ANY PIE—SWEET OR SAVORY**

roughly 7oz (200g) leftover puff pastry off-cuts, defrosted if frozen, and rolled out thinly
1 egg, beaten

1  Cut your rolled-out puff pastry into small pieces, roughly 2 in (5 cm) square. Lay these, overlapping on top of your pie, starting from the edge and working inward. The idea is not to be too neat—they should be randomly placed and look rough and cobbled.

2  Once the pie is fully covered, brush with egg and bake for 25–30 minutes, until the top is gloriously golden and puffy.

**Note:** This is less a recipe and more a fun idea for a pie crust using up any leftover bits of pastry you have—useful if you've forgotten to buy pastry or can't be bothered to make your own, plus it is very forgiving since it's supposed to look messy and chunky.

# Sauces & Condiments

These flavorful sauces and condiments add an extra dimension to my upside-down tarts and pies, and while versions of them can easily be store-bought, it's always nice if you can find the time to prepare your own. They're all easy to make, and once you've tried homemade it's hard to go back.

## Slow-Cooked Tomato Sauce
**MAKES ROUGHLY 1¼ CUPS (300ML)**

½ onion, finely chopped
drizzle of extra-virgin olive oil
2 garlic cloves, finely grated
1 tsp chopped fresh oregano, divided
1 tsp dried oregano
2 (14.5oz/400g) cans chopped tomatoes
1¼ cups (300ml) vegetable stock
1 tsp tomato paste
1 tbsp balsamic vinegar
splash of dry white wine
pinch of sugar
salt and freshly ground black pepper

1   Sauté the onion in a little olive oil in a large saucepan on medium heat for roughly 6 minutes, until softened. Stir the onion often so it cooks evenly. Stir in the garlic, half of the fresh oregano, and all the dried oregano and cook gently for another 4 minutes, or until the onion starts to color.

2   Pour in the canned tomatoes, then refill the cans with the stock and add to the pan (to get all that tomato-y residue). Stir in the tomato paste, balsamic vinegar, white wine, and sugar, then season well with salt and pepper.

3   Allow the sauce to come to a boil, then turn the heat down to the lowest setting and let it gently bubble and simmer away for at least 2 hours, until thickened. It should reduce by half, if not more. Stir in the remaining fresh oregano at the end and let the sauce cool fully before use.

**Note:** This slow-cooked tomato sauce is my go-to—it works with so many dishes, from pasta and pizza, to serving with meatballs. Once made, it can be kept in the fridge for 1 week or frozen for up to 1 month.

## White Sauce
**MAKES ROUGHLY 2 CUPS (500ML)**

2 cups (500ml) milk (I used skim, but go with your preference)
3 tbsp (50g) all-purpose flour
3 tbsp (50g) salted butter
salt and freshly ground black pepper

1   Add the milk to a saucepan on medium heat and then add the flour and butter. Using a balloon whisk, gently whisk the sauce for about 3 minutes, until it begins to thicken, then continue whisking until lusciously creamy and thick, roughly another 3 minutes.

2   Turn the heat to its lowest setting and cook the sauce for a further 5 minutes, whisking every so often to ensure it doesn't stick on the bottom. Stir in a little salt and pepper to taste. The sauce is now ready to use or be turned into a cheese sauce (see below).

**Note:** This all-in-one method results in a classic white sauce, perfect for lasagna or fish pie, but you can dress it up by adding your favorite cheeses. For a light, creamy sauce, stir in 3½oz (100g) cream cheese when the white sauce has finished cooking. For a stronger-tasting sauce, add ¾ cup (85g) grated mature Cheddar and stir until melted.

**Introduction**

## Homemade Mayonnaise
**MAKES ROUGHLY 1 CUP (200ML)**

2 large egg yolks
1 heaped tsp Dijon mustard
½ tsp salt
1 tsp sugar
⅔ cup (140ml) cold-pressed canola oil
2 tsp white wine vinegar
1 tsp lemon juice

1. Place all the ingredients in a tall beaker or jar with 2 teaspoons of water. Place your immersion blender toward the bottom of the beaker or jar and blend on high speed. As the mayo starts to emulsify, slowly pull the blender upward. The ingredients for the mayonnaise will come together in a few seconds and become smooth and creamy.

2. Spoon the mayonnaise into a jar. It will keep for up to 3 days in the fridge.

**Note:** My favorite oil to use is cold-pressed canola oil, but a regular light olive oil is a good alternative. Try adding 2 cloves of peeled roasted garlic to the jar before you blend to make the most wonderful garlic mayonnaise.

## Tartar Sauce
**MAKES ROUGHLY 1¼ CUPS (300ML)**

2 large egg yolks
1 tbsp Dijon mustard
1 cup (250ml) extra-virgin olive oil
2 tsp white wine vinegar
1 cornichon, chopped
1 tbsp capers
1 tsp lemon juice
1 tbsp chopped parsley leaves
2 tsp chopped tarragon leaves

1. Blend the egg yolks, Dijon mustard, olive oil, and vinegar in a jar with an immersion blender until emulsified into a mayonnaise-like consistency.

2. Add the rest of the ingredients and pulse briefly a few times to combine and until you have a thick tartar sauce. It will keep, covered, for up to 3 days in the fridge.

## Pesto
**MAKES ROUGHLY 1¼ CUPS (300ML)**

⅓ cup (50g) pine nuts
1 bunch of fresh basil, including stalks, roughly 3oz (85g)
1¾oz (50g) Parmesan, finely grated
⅔ cup (150ml) extra-virgin olive oil
2 garlic cloves, peeled

1. Heat a small skillet over low heat. Add the pine nuts and toast, shaking the pan occasionally, until golden. You want to avoid them burning. Let the nuts cool.

2. Put the nuts into a food processor with the basil, Parmesan, oil, and garlic and blitz until almost smooth. It will keep, covered, for up to 3 days in the fridge.

**Note:** Replace the pine nuts with pistachios or walnuts. Use arugula instead of basil for a peppery flavor. A strong, crumbly Cheddar also works well in place of the Parmesan.

# Individual Tarts & Pies

It's said that we all have about five go-to dishes in our cooking repertoire, ones we make on repeat—and there's nothing wrong with that! These dishes are always a hit with friends and family, you know they'll get eaten, they're simple to prepare, and they deliver on taste every time. I'm exactly the same, but my five dishes are big meals and I wanted to add something to the list that I can bring out at the last minute for a quick lunch with a friend or a small, romantic meal for two. I'm looking for a bite to eat that I can hold in my hand to munch on the go, or stuff into a lunchbox and take to work. So, this chapter is all about those individual tarts and pies that come with the addition of my upside-down twist. And, of course, I want to keep it simple; if one of these creations is going to make it into my top five go-to meals, then it has to be as easy as grabbing a sheet of puff pastry and layering it on top of whatever filling ingredient is in the fridge, creating something stunningly delicious.

# Shallot & Cream Cheese Tarts

If you've got this far into the book and still aren't quite sure what all the fuss is about, then maybe these little tarts will clear things up. This is the tart that started it all. The one that went viral on social media and turned my life (as well as my cooking) upside down. It's such a simple idea, layering shallots onto seasoned oil and then covering them with a cream-cheese-slathered sheet of puff pastry. I mean, what's not to love about sweet roasted shallots with a velvety, creamy topping and crisp, golden puff pastry?

## Makes 8

2 premade 9¾ x 10½ in sheets
   of puff pastry or use
   homemade (see p.12) rolled
   to 14 x 9 in (35 x 23 cm)
drizzle of extra-virgin olive oil
drizzle of balsamic vinegar
2 sprigs of thyme, leaves
   picked, plus extra to serve
salt and freshly ground
   black pepper
8 shallots, peeled and cut in
   half lengthwise
1¾oz (50g) herb cream cheese
1 egg, beaten

### YOU WILL NEED
large sheet pan, roughly
   15 x 10½ in (38 x 27 cm),
   lined with parchment paper

**1** Preheat the oven to 425°F (220°C). Remove the pastry from the fridge and set aside.

**2** Mark out 8 rectangles on the parchment paper, roughly 4½ x 3½ in (11 x 8.5 cm), leaving space between each one. Place the parchment paper back on the pan, drawn side down. (You can use 2 sheet pans if easier, dividing the paper in half.) Drizzle a little olive oil and balsamic vinegar on each rectangle, then sprinkle with the thyme. Season with salt and pepper. Top with the shallots, cut-side down—I use 2 halves per tart.

**3** Roll out the puff pastry and divide into 8 rectangles, roughly the same size as the ones drawn on the parchment paper. Slather one side of each piece of pastry with a generous teaspoon of cream cheese, leaving a narrow border around the edge. Lay the pastry, cream cheese side down, over each pair of shallots. Using the back of a fork, press indentations around the edges of the pastry to seal. Score a cross diagonally on the top of each one with a sharp knife and then brush with egg.

**4** Bake for 25–30 minutes, until the pastry is wonderfully golden and puffy. Remove from the oven and allow the tarts to sit on the pan for 5 minutes before flipping them over with a spatula. Sprinkle with a little extra thyme before serving.

**Individual Tarts & Pies**

# Tuna Melt Tarts

My dad lives in California and we visit him regularly. There's something magical about the glamour of Hollywood, the beach lifestyle, and the wonderful drive from LA up the Pacific Coast Highway to Sonoma where Dad lives. On the drive there is a restaurant tucked away in the hills of Big Sur called Nepenthe with stunning views of the Pacific ocean—and the best tuna melt sandwich you will ever eat. If you can't get to Nepenthe, try my twist on the classic.

## Makes 6

2 premade 9¾ x 10½ in sheets of puff pastry or use homemade (see p.12) rolled to 14 x 9 in (35 x 23 cm)
drizzle of extra-virgin olive oil
2 tbsp chopped dill, divided, plus extra to serve
3½oz (100g) Cheddar cheese, finely grated, divided
2 (5oz/160g) cans tuna in olive oil
1 celery stalk, finely chopped
3 green onions, finely chopped
1 cornichon, finely chopped
1 tsp horseradish sauce
2 tbsp Mayonnaise (see p.17), or use premade
juice of ½ lemon
salt and freshly ground black pepper
1 egg, beaten

### YOU WILL NEED
large sheet pan, roughly 15 x 10½ in (38 x 27 cm), lined with parchment paper

**1** Preheat the oven to 425°F (220°C). Remove the pastry from the fridge and set aside.

**2** Mark out 6 squares on the sheet of parchment paper, roughly 4½ in (11 cm) square, leaving space between each one. Place the parchment paper back on the pan, drawn side down. Drizzle a little olive oil on each square.

**3** Leaving a ½-in (1-cm) border, sprinkle half of the chopped dill on the squares and a quarter of the grated Cheddar.

**4** In a large bowl, mix the tuna, celery, green onions, cornichon, horseradish sauce, mayonnaise, and lemon juice with half of the remaining Cheddar and the remaining dill until combined. Season with salt and pepper. Spoon a generous tablespoon of the tuna mixture in the middle of each square, then sprinkle the rest of the cheese on top.

**5** Roll out the puff pastry, laying it horizontally on the worktop. Cut the pastry into 6 squares, roughly the same size as the ones drawn on the parchment paper, and lay them over the tuna mixture. Using your fingers, press down the edges of the pastry to seal. Score a cross diagonally on the top of each one with a sharp knife and then brush with egg.

**6** Bake for 15 minutes, then turn the oven down to 350°F (180°C) and cook for a further 10 minutes, or until the pastry is wonderfully golden and puffy. Remove from the oven and allow the tarts to sit on the pan for 5 minutes before flipping them over with a spatula. Sprinkle with extra dill before serving.

**Individual Tarts & Pies**

# Cheesy Potato Tarts

If there are two things in my life I could never give up, it would be cheese and potatoes. They're the ultimate in comfort food, and then you add crispy, golden puff pastry into the mix and you're on to a winner. I defy any cheese-lover not to adore these little tarts of joy.

## Makes 2

2 premade 9¾ x 10½ in sheets of puff pastry or use homemade (see p.12) rolled to 14 x 9 in (35 x 23 cm)
2 unpeeled white potatoes, cut into ½-in- (1-cm-) thick slices
drizzle of extra-virgin olive oil
2 sprigs of rosemary, leaves picked, divided
salt and freshly ground black pepper
3½oz (100g) Gruyere cheese, finely grated, divided
3½oz (100g) garlic and herb cream cheese
1 egg, beaten

### YOU WILL NEED
large sheet pan, roughly 15 x 10½ in (38 x 27 cm), lined with parchment paper

**1** Preheat the oven to 425°F (220°C). Remove the pastry from the fridge and set aside.

**2** Cook the sliced potatoes in gently boiling salted water for roughly 5 minutes. You want them to be tender but not so soft that they fall apart. Drain well and pat the potatoes dry with paper towels. Set aside.

**3** Mark out 2 rectangles on the sheet of parchment paper, roughly 6½ x 9 in (17 x 23 cm), leaving space between each one. Place the parchment paper back on the pan, drawn side down. Drizzle a little olive oil on each rectangle, then sprinkle with half of the rosemary and season with salt and pepper.

**4** Leaving a ½-in (1-cm) border, sprinkle half of the grated Gruyere over the herby oil. Lay the potatoes on top of each rectangle in 2 overlapping rows, then sprinkle the rest of the cheese and rosemary on top.

**5** Roll out the puff pastry and cut into 2 rectangles, roughly the same size as the ones drawn on the parchment paper. Slather each piece of pastry with the garlic and herb cream cheese, leaving a narrow border around the edge. Lay the pastry, cream cheese side down, over the potatoes. Using your fingers, press down the edges of the pastry to seal. Score the top of each one in a diamond pattern with a sharp knife and then brush with egg.

**6** Bake for 15 minutes, then turn the oven down to 350°F (180°C) and cook for a further 10 minutes, or until the pastry is wonderfully golden and puffy. Remove from the oven and allow the tarts to sit on the pan for 5 minutes before placing a cutting board on top and flipping them over. Peel off the parchment paper before serving.

**Individual Tarts & Pies**

# Sesame Shrimp Toast Tarts

For me, nothing beats the memory of driving home from the local Chinese restaurant with a white plastic bag tightly wrapped around boxes of salt and pepper ribs, chicken and cashew stir-fry and, of course, shrimp toast. I'm not sure how authentic it was but, my word, the sweet gingery shrimp on deep-fried crunchy toast were just the best. This puff pastry version works great here, especially if you can find a premade all-butter puff pastry.

**Makes 6**

2 premade 9¾ x 10½ in sheets of puff pastry or use homemade (see p.12) rolled to 14 x 9 in (35 x 23 cm)
drizzle of extra-virgin olive oil
drizzle of sesame oil
1 tbsp sesame seeds or a seed mix
½lb (200g) raw large shrimp, peeled and deveined
1 2-in piece of fresh ginger, roughly chopped
2 garlic cloves, peeled
1 egg white
1 tbsp soy sauce
1 tsp sugar
1 egg, beaten
3 green onions, sliced diagonally, to garnish

**YOU WILL NEED**
large sheet pan, roughly 15 x 10½ in (38 x 27 cm), lined with parchment paper

**1** Preheat the oven to 425°F (220°C). Remove the pastry from the fridge and set aside.

**2** Mark out 6 squares on the sheet of parchment paper, each roughly 4½ in (11 cm) square, leaving space between each one. Place the parchment paper back on the pan, drawn side down. Drizzle a liberal amount of olive oil and sesame oil on each square, then sprinkle with the sesame seeds or seed mix.

**3** In a food processor, whiz the shrimp, ginger, garlic, egg white, soy sauce, and sugar to a smooth paste.

**4** Roll out the puff pastry, laying it horizontally on the worktop. Cut the pastry into 6 squares, roughly the same size as the ones drawn on the parchment paper. Slather one side of each pastry square generously with the shrimp paste, leaving a narrow border around the edge. Lay the pastry, paste side down, over the seeds. Using the back of a fork, press indentations around the pastry to seal. Score the top of each one in a diamond pattern with a sharp knife and then brush with egg.

**5** Bake for 30–35 minutes, until the pastry is wonderfully golden and puffy. Remove from the oven and allow the tarts to sit on the pan for 5 minutes before flipping them over with a spatula. Sprinkle with the sliced green onions, then cut each one into 2 triangles to serve.

# Asparagus & Ibérico Ham Tarts

When we were kids, asparagus was a rather sophisticated vegetable. Hard to find in the supermarkets and expensive to order in a restaurant, where it was usually eaten with hushed reverence dipped in melted butter or hollandaise sauce. Mum would throw dinner parties and serve a few asparagus spears on a plate with butter and that was fancy. Now, when asparagus season rolls around there seems to be an abundance—perfect for making these tarts, which have a wonderful retro feel.

## Makes 2

2 premade 9¾ x 10½ in sheets of puff pastry or use homemade (see p.12) rolled to 14 x 9 in (35 x 23 cm)
drizzle of extra-virgin olive oil
drizzle of balsamic vinegar
roughly 1 tbsp chives, snipped
salt and freshly ground black pepper
16 thin asparagus spears, trimmed
8 slices of Ibérico ham (or another cured ham), cut in half lengthwise
4½oz (125g) brie, cut into thin slices
1 egg, beaten

### YOU WILL NEED
large sheet pan, roughly 15 x 10½ in (38 x 27 cm), lined with parchment paper

**1** Preheat the oven to 425°F (220°C). Remove the pastry from the fridge and set aside.

**2** Mark out 2 rectangles on the sheet of parchment paper, roughly 6½ x 9 in (17 x 23 cm), leaving space between each one. Place the parchment paper back on the pan, drawn side down. Drizzle a little olive oil and balsamic vinegar on the rectangles, then sprinkle with the chives and season with salt and pepper.

**3** Wrap each asparagus spear in a slice of ham. Place the spears slightly spaced apart horizontally on the herby oil, leaving a border around the edge. I use 8 ham-wrapped asparagus spears for each tart. Lay the slices of brie on top.

**4** Roll out the puff pastry and cut it into 2 rectangles, roughly the same size as the ones drawn on the parchment paper. Lay the pastry over the brie. Using your fingers, press down the edges of the pastry to seal. Score the top of each one in a diamond pattern with a sharp knife and then brush with egg.

**5** Bake for 25 minutes, or until the pastry is wonderfully golden and puffy. Remove from the oven and allow the tarts to sit on the pan for 5 minutes before flipping them over with a spatula. Serve as tarts or slap them together for the perfect crunchy asparagus and ham sandwich.

**Individual Tarts & Pies**

# Sausage, Tomato, & Bean Tarts

These little tarts are like an "open" version of my favorite snack, the sausage roll. Ridiculously easy to make, you simply mash everything together with the sausage and then lay the pastry over the top. They would be the perfect warming bite to eat while standing outside on a chilly fall evening around a bonfire.

## Makes 6

2 premade 9¾ x 10½ in sheets of puff pastry or use homemade (see p.12) rolled to 14 x 9 in (35 x 23 cm)
drizzle of extra-virgin olive oil
2 sprigs of thyme, leaves picked
salt and freshly ground black pepper
4 good-quality pork sausages
2 tbsp canned lima beans
2½oz (75g) Cheddar cheese, grated
1 tbsp Slow-Cooked Tomato Sauce (see p.16), plus extra to serve, or use premade
1 egg, beaten

### YOU WILL NEED
large sheet pan, roughly 15 x 10½ in (38 x 27 cm), lined with parchment paper
4-in (10-cm) round cookie cutter, ramekin, or bowl

1  Preheat the oven to 425°F (220°C). Remove the pastry from the fridge and set aside.

2  Using a 4-in (10-cm) cookie cutter, ramekin, or bowl as a template, draw 6 circles onto the parchment paper, leaving space between each one. Place the parchment paper back on the pan, drawn side down. Drizzle a little olive oil on each circle, then sprinkle with the thyme and season with salt and pepper.

3  In a large bowl, squeeze the sausages out of their skins, then mix in the lima beans, Cheddar, and tomato sauce with a fork. Don't overmix; you want some crushed beans and some whole ones. Set aside.

4  Leaving a ½-in (1-cm) border, spoon a tablespoon of the sausage mixture in the middle of each circle.

5  Roll out the puff pastry and, using the same cookie cutter, ramekin, or bowl, cut out 6 disks. (Save any leftover pastry to use in another recipe, see pp.14–15.) Lay the pastry disks over the sausage mixture. Using your fingers, press down the edges of the pastry to seal. Score the top of each one in a crisscross pattern with a sharp knife and then brush with egg.

6  Bake for 15 minutes, then turn the oven down to 350°F (180°C) and cook for a further 10 minutes, or until the pastry is wonderfully golden and puffy. Remove from the oven and allow the tarts to sit on the pan for 5 minutes before flipping them over with a spatula. Serve with small bowlfuls of the slow-cooked tomato sauce.

**Individual Tarts & Pies**

# Serrano Ham, Mozzarella, & Pesto Tarts

These little tarts remind me of Mediterranean vacations, and in the depth of a British winter this is always a good thing. I love that you can have them on the table in around 30 minutes with very little effort, and the whole house will have the aroma of an Italian cantina. There's also something ridiculously fancy about anything draped in puff pastry, and if you leave these tarts on the tray to flip over in front of your guests before serving, then they will think you're some kind of professionally trained chef—that's a win in my book.

**Makes 6**

2 premade 9¾ x 10½ in sheets of puff pastry or use homemade (see p.12) rolled to 14 x 9 in (35 x 23 cm)
drizzle of extra-virgin olive oil
½ red onion, thinly sliced
2 tsp dried oregano
salt and freshly ground black pepper
4½oz (125g) ball of mozzarella, drained and torn into small pieces
12 slices of Serrano ham (or another cured ham)
3 tbsp Pesto (see p.17), or use premade
1 egg, beaten

**YOU WILL NEED**
large sheet pan, roughly 15 x 10½ in (38 x 27 cm), lined with parchment paper

1   Preheat the oven to 425°F (220°C). Remove the pastry from the fridge and set aside.

2   Mark out 6 squares on the sheet of parchment paper, each roughly 4½ in (11 cm) square, leaving space between each one. Place the parchment paper back on the pan, drawn side down. Drizzle a little olive oil on each square.

3   Leaving a ½-in (1-cm) border, arrange a few slices of onion on top of each square. Sprinkle with the oregano and season with salt and pepper. Top with the mozzarella, followed by the slices of Serrano ham, gathering it to fit. I use 2 slices of ham for each tart.

4   Roll out the puff pastry, laying it horizontally on the worktop. Cut the pastry into 6 squares, roughly the same size as the ones drawn on the parchment paper. Spread a teaspoon of pesto over one side of each pastry square, leaving a narrow border. Lay the pastry, pesto side down, over the ham and mozzarella. Using your fingers, press down the edges of the pastry to seal. Score the top of each one in a diamond pattern with a sharp knife and then brush with egg.

5   Bake for 15 minutes, then turn the oven down to 350°F (180°C) and cook for a further 10 minutes, or until the pastry is wonderfully golden and puffy. Remove from the oven and allow the tarts to sit on the pan for 5 minutes before flipping them over with a spatula to serve.

**Individual Tarts & Pies**

# Mini Puff Pizzas

Pizza makes everyone happy, and these little beauties are perfect for so many occasions: a kid's party, speedy weekday dinner with the family, or even games night. I've gone for classic pepperoni but the choice of toppings is endless. I often lay out a good selection of toppings and let everyone build their own pizza—the kids love it so much, and it suits picky adults! They also love the big flip and final reveal.

**Makes 6**

2 premade 9¾ x 10½ in sheets of puff pastry or use homemade (see p.12) rolled to 14 x 9 in (35 x 23 cm)
drizzle of extra-virgin olive oil
½ red onion, thinly sliced
1 tsp dried oregano
salt and freshly ground black pepper
18 slices of pepperoni, roughly 3 per tart
¾ cup (100g) shredded mozzarella
4 tbsp Slow-Cooked Tomato Sauce (see p.16), or use premade
1 egg, beaten

**YOU WILL NEED**
large sheet pan, roughly 15 x 10½ in (38 x 27 cm), lined with parchment paper
4-in (10-cm) round cookie cutter, ramekin, or bowl

**1** Preheat the oven to 350°F (180°C). Remove the pastry from the fridge and set aside.

**2** Using a 4-in (10-cm) cookie cutter, ramekin, or bowl as a template, draw 6 circles onto the parchment paper, leaving space between each one. Place the parchment paper back on the pan, drawn side down. Drizzle a little olive oil on each circle.

**3** Leaving a ½-in (1-cm) border, arrange a few slices of onion on top of each circle, then sprinkle with oregano. Season with salt and pepper. Top with the slices of pepperoni and finish with a sprinkling of mozzarella.

**4** Roll out the puff pastry and, using the same cookie cutter, ramekin, or bowl, cut out 6 disks. (Save any leftover pastry to use in another recipe, see pp.14–15.) Slather one side of each pastry disk with tomato sauce, leaving a narrow border around the edge. Lay the pastry disks, sauce side down, over the pepperoni and mozzarella mixture. Using your fingers, press down the edges of the pastry to seal. Score the top of each one in a crisscross pattern with a sharp knife and then brush with egg.

**5** Bake for 35 minutes, or until the pastry is wonderfully golden and puffy. Remove from the oven and allow the pizzas to sit on the pan for 4 minutes before flipping them over with a spatula to serve.

**Individual Tarts & Pies**

# Upside Down Vegetable Samosas

Up there with the Cornish pasty, the Greek spanakopita or the South American empanada, the Indian samosa is, in my opinion, one of the best handheld pies. Packed with spices and veggies, they can be made in a big batch and will keep for a few days. They're also vegan, and I've been saved many times by these little treats following a surprise visit from a vegetarian or vegan friend.

**Makes 8**

4 premade 9¾ x 10½ in sheets of puff pastry or use 2 batches homemade (see p.12) each rolled to 14 x 9 in (35 x 23 cm)
2 potatoes, peeled and diced
1 small carrot, diced
1 onion, diced
½ cup (75g) frozen peas
½ tsp cumin seeds
1 green chile, finely chopped
1 2-in piece of fresh ginger, peeled and grated
¼ tsp ground turmeric
pinch of salt
1 tsp ground coriander
1 tsp garam masala
½ tsp dried chili flakes
drizzle of extra-virgin olive oil
2 tbsp mango chutney
1 egg, beaten
2 tsp coriander seeds, for sprinkling

**YOU WILL NEED**
2 large sheet pans, roughly 15 x 10½ in (38 x 27 cm), lined with parchment paper
cardboard triangle template, roughly 6 x 6 x 6 in (15 x 15 x 15 cm)

**1** Preheat the oven to 425°F (220°C). Remove the pastry from the fridge and set aside.

**2** Using the cardboard triangle as a template, mark out 4 triangles on each sheet of parchment paper. Place the parchment paper back on the pans, drawn side down.

**3** Cook the potatoes and carrot in a pan of boiling salted water for 5 minutes, until just tender. Drain well and place the vegetables in a large bowl with the rest of the ingredients up to and including the olive oil. Add a splash of water and mix well until everything is combined.

**4** Drizzle a little extra olive oil on the drawn triangles, then top each one with a tablespoon of the samosa filling, placing it in the middle and spreading it out slightly into a triangle, leaving a border all the way around.

**5** Roll out the puff pastry and, using the same cardboard template as before, cut out 8 triangles. (Save any leftover pastry to use in another recipe, see pp.14–15.) Spread a dollop of mango chutney on each pastry triangle, leaving a border around the edge. Lay the pastry, chutney side down, over the samosa filling. Using the back of a fork, press indentations around the edges of the pastry to seal. Score the top of each one in a diamond pattern with a sharp knife and then brush with egg. Sprinkle the coriander seeds on top.

**6** Bake for 30 minutes, until the pastry is golden and puffy. Remove from the oven and let the samosas sit on the pans for 5 minutes before flipping them over with a spatula to serve.

**Individual Tarts & Pies**

# Sausage, Red Onion, & Mustard Tarts

These are another of my favorite sausage tarts, but this time I use pie crust instead of puff pastry. If you're a parent or come from a large family, or are generally short on time, you'll know how handy sausages are—fry 'em, bake 'em, grill 'em, use the insides to make meatballs, serve them with mashed potatoes and gravy, bake them in batter—they're so convenient and versatile I make no apologies for using them a lot. What's more, they really work well with upside-down bakes because they are always ready in next to no time.

**Makes 6**

1 recipe of homemade pie
   dough (see p.13) rolled
   out to roughly 14 x 9 in
   (35 x 23 cm)
2 tbsp chili oil
drizzle of balsamic vinegar
salt and freshly ground
   black pepper
½ red onion, thinly sliced
6 good-quality pork sausages,
   cut in half lengthwise
3 tbsp Dijon mustard
1 egg, beaten

**YOU WILL NEED**
large sheet pan, roughly
   15 x 10½ in (38 x 27 cm),
   lined with parchment paper

1  Preheat the oven to 425°F (220°C). Remove the pastry from the fridge and set aside.

2  Mark out 6 rectangles on the sheet of parchment paper, roughly 4½ x 3½ in (11 x 8.5cm), leaving space between each one. Place the parchment paper back on the pan, drawn side down. Drizzle the chili oil generously on each rectangle, followed by a little balsamic vinegar, then season with salt and pepper.

3  Leaving a ½-in (1-cm) border, place the sliced onion on top of the seasoned oil, followed by the sausage halves, placing them cut-side down. I use 2 sausage halves per tart.

4  Roll out the pie dough and cut it into 6 rectangles, roughly the same size as the ones drawn on the parchment paper. (Save any leftover pastry for another recipe, see pp.14–15.) Slather one side of each pastry rectangle with a generous teaspoonful of Dijon mustard, leaving a narrow border around the edge. Lay the pastry, mustard side down, over the sausages. Using the back of a fork, press indentations around the edge of the pastry to seal. Score 3–4 lines over the top of each one with a sharp knife and then brush with egg.

5  Bake for 35 minutes, or until the pastry is golden and crisp. Remove from the oven and let the tarts sit on the pan for 4 minutes before flipping them over with a spatula to serve.

**Individual Tarts & Pies**

# Carrot, Cilantro, & Feta Tarts

We live in a little cottage tucked away in the heart of the Lincolnshire Wolds. Our nearest town is 10 miles away. It's very rural and I was a little worried when we moved here full-time from London, mostly about sourcing some of the fancier foods I love. As it happens, another small village not too far away has the most incredible grocery store that stocks everything, and if they don't have it they will get it for you within 24 hours—like the tricolored carrots for this tart.

## Makes 2

2 premade 9¾ x 10½ in sheets of puff pastry or use homemade (see p.12) rolled to 14 x 9 in (35 x 23 cm)

7oz (200g) feta, divided

1 handful of cilantro (sub with basil if you're not a fan), plus extra to serve

1 tbsp extra-virgin olive oil, plus extra for drizzling

salt and freshly ground black pepper

2 sprigs of rosemary, leaves picked

roughly 6 tricolor carrots, sliced in half lengthwise (if using regular carrots cut them into long batons)

1 egg, beaten

### YOU WILL NEED

large sheet pan, roughly 15 x 10½ in (38 x 27 cm), lined with parchment paper

**1** Preheat the oven to 425°F (220°C). Remove the pastry from the fridge and set aside.

**2** Blend the feta, saving a little to sprinkle over at the end, and the cilantro in a mini food processor with the olive oil until smooth and pale green. Season with salt and pepper, then set aside.

**3** Mark out 2 rectangles on the sheet of parchment paper, roughly 6½ x 9 in (17 x 23 cm), leaving space between each one. Place the parchment paper back on the pan, drawn side down. Drizzle a little olive oil on each rectangle, sprinkle with half of the rosemary, then season with salt and pepper.

**4** Leaving a ½-in (1-cm) border, place the carrot halves lengthwise on each of the rectangles.

**5** Roll out the puff pastry and make 2 rectangles. Slather one side of each piece of pastry with the whipped feta and cilantro mixture, leaving a narrow border around the edge. Lay the pastry, cheese-side down, over the top of the carrots. Using the back of a fork, press indentations around the edge of the pastry to seal. Score the top of each one in a diamond pattern with a sharp knife and then brush with egg.

**6** Bake for 35 minutes, or until the pastry is wonderfully golden and puffy. Remove from the oven and let the tarts sit on the pan for 5 minutes, then lay a piece of parchment paper on top followed by a cutting board or plate and carefully flip them over. Peel off the backing paper. Sprinkle the remaining rosemary and feta on top of the tarts before serving.

**Individual Tarts & Pies**

# Chicken Tikka Pies

Saturday nights wouldn't be the same without a curry. It's been a tradition in our family for decades and, of course, we all have our favorite. I have a sweet spot in my heart for chicken tikka and I really wanted to capture its flavor in pie form. These are so good—the pastry turns crisp around the edges and has a wonderful golden glaze from the chutney.

**Makes 4**

3 boneless, skinless chicken thighs, cut into bite-size pieces
1 recipe of homemade pie dough (see p.13) rolled out to roughly 14 x 9 in (35 x 23 cm)
drizzle of extra-virgin olive oil
4 tbsp tomato chutney
1 egg, beaten
1 tsp fennel seeds

**For marinade 1:**
juice of 1 lemon
1 2-in piece of fresh ginger, peeled and finely grated
3 garlic cloves, finely grated
pinch each of salt and freshly ground black pepper

**For marinade 2:**
3 tbsp plain yogurt
1 tsp ground cumin
1 tsp ground coriander
1 tsp freshly ground black pepper
1 tsp medium chili powder
½ tsp ground turmeric
1 tsp garlic salt
1 handful of cilantro, leaves finely chopped

**YOU WILL NEED**
large sheet pan, roughly 15 x 10½ in (38 x 27 cm), lined with parchment paper
4-in (10-cm) round cookie cutter, ramekin, or bowl

1 In a large bowl, mix together the ingredients for marinade 1. Stir in the chicken and set aside for no more than 15 minutes, while you make the second marinade.

2 Place all the ingredients for marinade 2 in a second bowl and mix well. Once the chicken has had 15 minutes in the first marinade, pour the second marinade over the top and combine well. Cover the bowl with plastic wrap and pop it in the fridge for a minimum of 30 minutes or up to 24 hours.

3 Preheat the oven to 425°F (220°C). Remove the pastry from the fridge and set aside.

4 Using your 4-in (10-cm) cookie cutter, ramekin, or bowl as a template, draw 4 circles onto the parchment paper, leaving space between each one. Place the parchment paper back on the pan, drawn side down. Drizzle a little olive oil on each circle.

5 Leaving a ½-in (1-cm) border, spoon a generous heap of the marinated chicken in the middle of each circle.

6 Roll out the pie dough and, using the same cookie cutter, ramekin, or bowl, cut out 4 disks of pastry. (Save any leftover pastry for another recipe, see pp.14–15.) Spread a little chutney on one side of each disk, leaving a narrow border. Lay the pastry, chutney side down, over the chicken. Using the back of a fork, press indentations around the edge of the pastry to seal. Score a cross over the top of each one with a sharp knife and then brush with egg. Sprinkle the fennel seeds on top of each one.

7 Bake for 35 minutes, or until the pastry is golden and crisp. Remove from the oven and let the tarts sit on the pan for 3 minutes before flipping them over with a spatula to serve.

**Individual Tarts & Pies**

**44**

# Upside Down Cornish Pasties

The Cornish can be very particular when it comes to tradition (just ask which goes first on a scone—jam or cream!) and rightly so. Yet, I could hardly present you a book filled with pastry recipes and not deliver my upside-down take on the famous pasty. I've kept the filling 100 percent authentically classic, because why mess with perfection (and I don't want to upset anyone). You can obviously adapt the filling at your pleasure, but just keep it quiet!

**Makes 6**

1 recipe of homemade pie
   dough (see p.13) rolled
   out to roughly 14 x 9 in
   (35 x 23 cm)
5½oz (150g) white potato,
   peeled and diced
2½oz (75g) rutabaga, peeled
   and diced
7oz (200g) skirt steak, cut into
   small cubes
¼ cup (75g) thinly sliced onion
salt and freshly ground
   black pepper
drizzle of extra-virgin olive oil
1 egg, beaten

**YOU WILL NEED**

2 large sheet pans, roughly
   15 x 10½ in (38 x 27 cm)
   each, lined with parchment
   paper
8½-in (22-cm) round plate

1   Preheat the oven to 220°C (425°F). Remove the pastry from the fridge and set aside.

2   Cook the potato and rutabaga in a pan of boiling water for 5 minutes, until just tender (steaming works well here too). Drain the cooked vegetables well and place in a large bowl with the beef and onion. Season with plenty of salt and pepper and mix well.

3   Using the plate as a template, draw 3 semicircles on each sheet of parchment paper, leaving space between each one. Place the parchment paper back on the pans, drawn side down. Drizzle a little olive oil on the semicircles, then season with salt and pepper.

4   Leaving a ½-in (1-cm) border, spoon the mixed vegetables and meat mixture in a pile within each drawn semicircle.

5   Roll out the pie dough and, using the same plate as before, cut out 6 semicircular shapes. (Save any leftover pastry for another recipe, see pp.14–15.) Lay the pastry over the pasty filling. Using your fingers, press down the edges of the pastry to seal (the curved edge can be crimped to resemble a traditional Cornish pasty, if you like). Brush the top of each one with egg and pierce a hole in the top with a skewer.

6   Bake for 30 minutes, or until the pastry is golden and crisp. Remove from the oven and let the pasties sit on the pans for 5 minutes before flipping them over with a spatula to serve.

**Individual Tarts & Pies**

# Sharing is Caring

I grew up in a perfectly normal suburban family home. My childhood was lovely: two wonderful parents and an older brother who I wanted to kill on a regular basis! Thankfully, my brother Jason and I survived childhood and have grown into good friends, but back in the day if you had passed our childhood home at suppertime it's possible you would have heard us screaming bloody murder at each other as we fought over whether he had more roast potatoes than me, or if my slice of apple and blackberry pie was larger than his. You can imagine how exhausted my mother was at mealtimes! With this memory in mind, I wanted to create a collection of recipes for sharing that ensured equal portions for everyone. I also love a pie that you can place in the middle of the table, cut into slices and let everyone dig in. All the host has to do is hold their breath as they deftly flip the pie right side up to serve. Something that should be done in front of everyone for maximum dramatic effect.

# Beet, Red Onion, & Goat Cheese Tart

As a child I was traumatized by pickled beets. I had no idea they came any other way and I just couldn't stomach them. They were often served as limp, crinkle-cut slices along with a hunk of lettuce and a bland wedge of tomato and called "salad." But something changed as my tastes matured and I also realized that this humble root vegetable didn't have to come in a jar. Pickled, roasted, steamed, blended—I now absolutely adore beets, especially when they're slightly caramelized as in this tart. They also pair beautifully with red onion and goat cheese. This tart is what I'd call the ultimate "light lunch." Absolutely divine served warm out of the oven, or left to cool and eaten alongside a stunning salad.

## Serves 2–4

2 premade 9¾ x 10½ in sheets of puff pastry or use homemade (see p.12) rolled to 14 x 9 in (35 x 23 cm)
drizzle of extra-virgin olive oil
drizzle of honey, plus extra to serve
2 sprigs of thyme, leaves picked, divided
salt and freshly ground black pepper
1 red onion, thinly sliced
3 cooked medium-size beets, cut into thin wedges (I use the vacuum-packed kind, no vinegar)
4½oz (125g) soft goat cheese, divided
1 egg, beaten

**YOU WILL NEED**
large sheet pan, roughly 15 x 10½ in (38 x 27 cm), lined with parchment paper
8½-in (22-cm) round plate (it needs to fit on the pastry)

1  Preheat the oven to 425°F (220°C). Remove the pastry from the fridge and set aside.

2  Draw around the 8½-in (22-cm) plate on the parchment paper, then place it drawn side down on the sheet pan. Drizzle a little olive oil on the circle, followed by honey and a sprinkling of thyme, saving some to serve. Season with salt and pepper.

3  Leaving a ¾-in (2-cm) border, lay the onion slices on top of the drawn circle, then the beet wedges. I prefer a relaxed arrangement because I think it looks better, but feel free to create a pattern with your vegetables. Crumble half of the goat cheese on top and season with extra salt and pepper.

4  Roll out the puff pastry and, using the same plate as before, cut around it to make a disk. Lay the pastry disk over the top of the beets and goat cheese. Using the back of a fork, press indentations around the edge of the pastry to seal. Score the top in a diamond pattern with a sharp knife and then brush with egg.

5  Bake for 30 minutes, or until the pastry is wonderfully golden and puffy. Remove from the oven and allow the tart to sit on the pan for 5 minutes. Lay a piece of parchment paper on top, followed by a cutting board or plate, and carefully flip it over. Peel off the backing paper. You may want to slide the tart back onto the sheet pan and into the oven for a few minutes to get a little more golden on top.

6  To serve, crumble the remaining goat cheese on the top and drizzle with extra honey. Finish with the rest of the thyme leaves and season with salt and pepper.

**Sharing is Caring**

# Chicken Pot Pie

50

An absolutely classic family meal. This pie is pure comfort food, and any dish that features my favorite meat and veggies bathed in a rich, creamy cheese sauce has to be good. I promise this pie will make the call to dinner answered in a flash.

## Serves 4–6

2 premade 9¾ x 10½ in sheets of puff pastry or use homemade (see p.12) rolled to 14 x 9 in (35 x 23 cm)
drizzle of extra-virgin olive oil
1 sprig of thyme, leaves picked
1 sprig of rosemary, leaves picked
salt and freshly ground black pepper
handful of button mushrooms, cut in half
4 shallots, quartered
1 carrot, sliced diagonally
1 celery stalk, chopped
handful of frozen peas
leftover roast chicken meat, roughly ½lb (200g), shredded
½ recipe quantity of Cheesy Sauce (see p.54)
1 egg, beaten

### YOU WILL NEED
large sheet pan, roughly 15 x 10½ in (38 x 27 cm), lined with parchment paper

**1** Preheat the oven to 425°F (220°C). Remove the pastry from the fridge and set aside.

**2** Mark out a 14 x 9 in (35 x 23 cm) rectangle on the parchment paper and place it drawn side down on the sheet pan. Drizzle on a little olive oil, then sprinkle with the thyme and rosemary. Season with salt and pepper.

**3** Leaving a ¾-in (2-cm) border, lay the mushrooms, shallots, carrot, and celery on top of the rectangle, followed by the peas. I prefer a relaxed arrangement because I think it looks better, but feel free to create a pattern with your vegetables. Next, layer your shredded chicken on top and season with salt and pepper. Carefully pour over the Cheesy Sauce.

**4** Lay the puff pastry over the top of the saucy chicken and vegetables. Using the back of a fork, press indentations around the edge of the pastry to seal. Score the top in a diamond pattern with a sharp knife and then brush with egg.

**5** Bake for 35 minutes, or until the pastry is wonderfully golden and puffy. Remove from the oven and allow the pie to sit on the pan for 5 minutes. Lay a piece of parchment paper on top, followed by a cutting board or plate, and carefully flip the tart over. Peel off the backing paper. You may want to slide the tart back onto the sheet pan and into the oven for a few minutes to get a little more golden on top before serving.

**Note:** The wonderful thing about this pie is its versatility. Add the veggies you love or keep it vegetarian by swapping the chicken for sliced shiitake mushrooms.

**Sharing is Caring**

# Full English Breakfast Pie

A full English is a classic breakfast in the UK, and it can be quite a challenge to pull it all together. The timings are tricky and, of course, everyone has their particular preferences as to what should be on the plate. This is my "all-in-one" version, and each slice features a bit of everything. You can add your favorite items, such as black pudding, but I've gone with the stuff I love. Serve with a fried egg on top of each slice—what a glorious way to provide breakfast for the whole family.

## Serves 4–6

2 premade 9¾ x 10½ in sheets of puff pastry or use homemade (see p.12) rolled to 14 x 9 in (35 x 23 cm)
drizzle of extra-virgin olive oil
1 sprig of rosemary, leaves picked
salt and freshly ground black pepper
4 slices bacon, chopped
4 sausages, chopped
4 frozen hash browns, defrosted and chopped
handful of button mushrooms, cut into quarters
½ cup (150g) baked beans
1 egg, beaten

### YOU WILL NEED
large sheet pan, roughly 15 x 10½ in (38 x 27 cm), lined with parchment paper

**1** Preheat the oven to 220°C (425°F). Remove the pastry from the fridge and set aside.

**2** Mark out a 14 x 9 in (35 x 23 cm) rectangle on the parchment paper and place it drawn side down on the sheet pan. Drizzle on a little olive oil, then sprinkle with the rosemary and season with salt and pepper.

**3** Leaving a ½-in (1-cm) border, layer the chopped bacon, sausages, hash browns, mushrooms, and baked beans on top of the rectangle.

**4** Lay out the puff pastry and carefully drape it over the breakfast ingredients. Using the back of a fork, press indentations around the edge of the pastry to seal. Score the top in a diamond pattern with a sharp knife and then brush with egg.

**5** Bake for 35–40 minutes, or until the pastry is wonderfully golden and puffy. Remove from the oven and allow the pie to sit on the pan for 5 minutes. Lay a piece of parchment paper on top, followed by a cutting board or plate, and carefully flip the pie over. Peel off the backing paper before serving.

**Sharing is Caring**

# Upside Down Fish Pie

54

My grandparents on Mum's side were from the coastal city of Hull in Yorkshire, England, and were very fussy about fish. If ever they came down to London, they would always criticize the quality of the fish served in restaurants and how it could "never be as good as the fish from Hull." Grandma Jennie made a fish pie that was second to none with a glorious top of golden mashed potatoes. My recipe is inspired by hers but I'm replacing the mashed potatoes with puff pastry, which works as a beautiful alternative. The great thing about fish pie is that it's a really good way to encourage kids to eat fish.

## Serves 4–6

2 premade 9¾ x 10½ in sheets of puff pastry or use homemade (see p.12) rolled to 14 x 9 in (35 x 23 cm)
drizzle of extra-virgin olive oil
handful of dill, torn
salt and freshly ground black pepper
3 types of skinless fish, roughly 10oz (300g) in total, cut into bite-size chunks (I use a mix of salmon, hake, and smoked haddock)
5½oz (150g) large raw shrimp, peeled and deveined
⅔ cup (100g) frozen peas
1 egg, beaten

### For the cheesy sauce:
1 recipe quantity of White Sauce (see p.16)
3½oz (100g) sharp Cheddar cheese, grated
2 tbsp cream cheese

### YOU WILL NEED
large sheet pan, roughly 15 x 10½ in (38 x 27 cm), lined with parchment paper

**1** Start with the cheesy sauce. Make the white sauce following the instructions on page 16. Take the pan off the heat and stir in the Cheddar and cream cheese until combined. Set aside to cool slightly.

**2** Preheat the oven to 220°C (425°F). Remove the pastry from the fridge and set aside.

**3** Mark out a 14 x 9 in (35 x 23 cm) rectangle on the parchment paper and place it drawn side down on the sheet pan. Drizzle on a little olive oil, then sprinkle with the dill and season with salt and pepper.

**4** Leaving a ¾-in (2-cm) border, place your mixed fish on top of the drawn rectangle, followed by the shrimp, and then sprinkle on the peas. Pour on the cheesy sauce and season with extra salt and pepper.

**5** Lay the puff pastry over the top of the fish mixture. Using the back of a spoon, press indentations around the edge of the pastry to seal. Make scale shapes on top of the pastry (you can use one half of a cookie cutter to do this) and then brush with egg.

**6** Bake for 25 minutes, or until the pastry is wonderfully golden and puffy. Remove from the oven and allow the pie to sit on the pan for 5 minutes. Lay a piece of parchment paper on top, followed by a cutting board or plate, and carefully flip the tart over. Peel off the backing paper. You may want to slide the tart back onto the sheet pan and into the oven for a few minutes to get a little more golden on top.

**Sharing is Caring**

# French Onion Soup Tarte Tatin

French onion is my husband's (otherwise known as The Viking) favorite soup. If he's feeling under the weather or just in need of comfort food, I will make him a bowl of the darkly golden, sweet elixir. I wanted to re-create the wonderful flavors of the classic soup in a tart, and so we have gloriously caramelized, sweet shallots combined with nutty Gruyère cheese, all topped with flaky puff pastry. I am totally here for it!

## Serves 4–6

2 premade 9¾ x 10½ in sheets of puff pastry or use homemade (see p.12) rolled to 14 x 9 in (35 x 23 cm)
all-purpose flour, for dusting
2 tbsp (30g) butter
drizzle of extra-virgin olive oil
6–7 shallots, peeled and cut in half lengthwise, root ends trimmed
3 sprigs of rosemary, leaves picked
3 sprigs of thyme, leaves picked, divided
salt and freshly ground black pepper
1 tsp light brown sugar
2 tbsp balsamic vinegar
2oz (60g) Gruyere cheese, finely grated

### YOU WILL NEED
9-in (23-cm) heavy-bottomed, ovenproof skillet (make sure the handle is heat resistant)

1   Preheat the oven to 375°F (190°C). Remove the pastry from the fridge and set aside.

2   Dust your worktop with a little flour and roll out the pastry sheet a little larger—it needs to be a bit bigger than the skillet you're using. Place the skillet on top of the pastry and cut out a disk ½ in (1 cm) larger than the pan. Lay the pastry disk on a flat plate or cookie sheet and pop it back in the fridge while you prepare the shallots.

3   Heat the butter and olive oil in the skillet on medium heat. When the butter melts, lay the shallots cut side up in the pan and sprinkle with all the rosemary and most of the thyme, saving some to sprinkle on at the end, and sauté for roughly 7 minutes. Season with salt and pepper and sprinkle with the brown sugar.

4   Drizzle a little more olive oil on the shallots and then, using two forks, flip them over onto their cut sides, ensuring they are nicely packed together in the pan. Sauté the shallots for another 5 minutes, until softened and golden, then pour in the balsamic vinegar and let it bubble away for another 3 minutes. Take the pan off the heat and sprinkle in the grated Gruyere.

5   Taking care because the pan is hot, lay the pastry over the top of the shallots and carefully tuck the edge down into the side of the pan. It doesn't matter if it looks a bit messy and folded on top, no one will notice once the tarte is turned out.

6   Bake for 25–30 minutes, until the pastry is golden and puffy. Remove from the oven and allow the tarte to sit for 3 minutes, then place a cutting board or a large plate over the pan and carefully but confidently flip the pan over. Use one swift movement, and make sure you have a kitchen towel or oven mitts to protect your hands from the heat. Sprinkle with the rest of the thyme and serve.

**Sharing is Caring**

# Tomato, Feta, & Chive Tart

We're fortunate to spend a lot of time in Mallorca, and Sunday is market day in the old town of Pollença. If you've ever visited a traditional European market, you'll know how impossible it is to pass them without purchasing something, and this is where I buy the most incredible tomatoes. So many varieties, so many shapes, sizes, and colors, that whenever I see them I just can't resist. Large pink heirlooms, dark purple vine tomatoes, yellow plum tomatoes—I'm as obsessed with their color as I am their flavor. When tomatoes are that good you don't want to mess with them too much, so this simple tart is perfect.

## Serves 4–6

2 premade 9¾ x 10½ in sheets of puff pastry or use homemade (see p.12) rolled to 14 x 9 in (35 x 23 cm)
drizzle of extra-virgin olive oil
drizzle of balsamic vinegar
salt and freshly ground black pepper
handful of chives, preferably in flower, stalks finely chopped, divided
roughly 7oz (200g) of mixed, colorful tomatoes, large and small, thickly sliced
5½oz (150g) feta, divided
1 egg, beaten

### YOU WILL NEED
large sheet pan, roughly 15 x 10½ in (38 x 27 cm), lined with parchment paper

1   Preheat the oven to 425°F (220°C). Remove the pastry from the fridge and set aside.

2   Mark out a 14 x 9 in (35 x 23 cm) rectangle on the parchment paper and place it drawn side down on the sheet pan. Drizzle on a little olive oil and balsamic vinegar, then season with salt and pepper. Sprinkle with the chives and flowers, saving some to serve at the end.

3   Leaving a ½-in (1-cm) border, place the sliced tomatoes on top of the rectangle, then crumble on half of the feta.

4   Lay the puff pastry over the tomatoes and feta. Using the back of a fork, press indentations around the edge of the pastry to seal. Score the top in a diamond pattern with a sharp knife and then brush with egg.

5   Bake for 35 minutes, or until the pastry is golden and puffy. Remove from the oven and allow the tart to sit on the pan for 5 minutes. Lay a piece of parchment paper on top, followed by a cutting board or plate, and carefully flip the tart over. Peel off the backing paper. You may want to slide the tart back onto the sheet pan and into the oven for a few minutes to get a little more golden on top.

6   Sprinkle the rest of the feta and extra chives (with their flowers) on top before serving.

**Note:** If you have difficulty buying chives in flower it's well worth growing your own. Chives only flower once a year but their sweet, delicate flavor and pretty lilac color are unbeatable. If they're not available, then just use the stems.

# Hawaiian Pizza

**60**

The Hawaiian must be the world's most controversial pizza. While I'm sure traditionalists would reel in horror at the thought of topping a pizza with pineapple, it has become a favorite of many, and was invented by a Canadian pizza maker in the 1950s, who used a brand of canned pineapple with Hawaiian-style imagery. I came around to the idea upon discovering that the fruit works beautifully with salty ham. So, if you are already a fan, then you know what I'm talking about—if you're not, or you're unsure, then now's the time to jump on board with my upside-down Hawaiian pizza.

## Serves 4

2 premade 9¾ x 10½ in sheets of puff pastry or use homemade (see p.12) rolled to 14 x 9 in (35 x 23 cm)
drizzle of extra-virgin olive oil
1 tsp Italian seasoning
salt and freshly ground black pepper
5 slices of Serrano ham (or another cured ham), cut in half lengthwise
1 tbsp canned pineapple chunks
3½oz (100g) mozzarella cheese, drained and torn into pieces
¾ cup (100g) shredded mozzarella cheese
3 tbsp Slow-Cooked Tomato Sauce (see p.16), or use premade, divided
1 egg, beaten
handful of basil leaves, to finish

### YOU WILL NEED
large sheet pan, roughly 15 x 10½ in (38 x 27 cm), lined with parchment paper
8½-in (22-cm) round plate (it needs to fit on the pastry)

**1** Preheat the oven to 425°F (220°C). Remove the pastry from the fridge and set aside.

**2** Draw around the 8½-in (22-cm) plate onto the parchment paper, then place it drawn side down on the sheet pan. Drizzle on a little olive oil, sprinkle with the Italian seasoning, then season with salt and pepper.

**3** Leaving a ½-in (1-cm) border, layer the ham, pineapple, and the torn and shredded mozzarella on the circle, then add spoonfuls of the tomato sauce, saving half for later.

**4** Roll out the puff pastry and, using the same plate as before, cut around it to make a disk. Slather one side of the pastry disk with the remaining tomato sauce, leaving a narrow border around the edge. Lay the pastry disk, sauce side down, over the top of the pizza ingredients. Using the back of a fork, press indentations around the edge of the pastry to seal. Score the top in a diamond pattern with a sharp knife and then brush with egg.

**5** Bake for 35 minutes, or until the pastry is wonderfully golden and puffy. Remove from the oven and allow the pizza to sit on the pan for 5 minutes. Lay a piece of parchment paper on top, followed by a cutting board or plate, and carefully flip the pizza over. Peel off the backing paper. You may want to slide the pizza back onto the sheet pan and into the oven for a few minutes to get a little more golden on top. Sprinkle with the basil leaves before serving.

**Sharing is Caring**

# Cheesy Leek Tart

I think leeks are the unsung hero of the vegetable world. Cooked well, they are wonderfully sweet and have a mild onion taste that is really quite sophisticated (if you can refer to a vegetable as such). They also add a silky luxury to any dish, including this tart. Warning: there's a lot of butter in this recipe, because leeks love butter—it brings out their flavor and complements them so well.

**Serves 4-6**

2 premade 9¾ x 10½ in sheets of puff pastry or use homemade (see p.12) rolled to 14 x 9 in (35 x 23 cm)
drizzle of extra-virgin olive oil
10 tbsp (150g) butter, cut into small cubes, divided
1 sprig of thyme, leaves picked
salt and freshly ground black pepper
3 leeks, cut into ½-in (1-cm) batons
3½oz (100g) Gruyere cheese, finely grated
1 egg, beaten

**YOU WILL NEED**
large sheet pan, roughly 15 x 10½ in (38 x 27 cm), lined with parchment paper
8½-in (22-cm) round plate (it needs to fit on the pastry)

1 Preheat the oven to 425°F (220°C). Remove the pastry from the fridge and set aside.

2 Draw around the 8½-in (22-cm) plate onto the parchment paper, then place it drawn side down on the sheet pan. Drizzle on a little olive oil, then sprinkle with half of the butter and the thyme. Season with salt and pepper.

3 Leaving a ½-in (1-cm) border, stand the leek batons upright close together on top of the drawn circle, so they're on their ends like little soldiers. Add the remaining butter and sprinkle with the grated Gruyere.

4 Roll out the puff pastry and, using the same plate as before, cut around it to make a disk, then drape it over the leeks. Using your fingers, press around the edge of the pastry to seal. Score the top in a diamond pattern with a sharp knife and then brush with egg.

5 Bake for 15 minutes, then turn the oven down to 350°F (180°C) and cook for a further 10 minutes, or until the pastry is wonderfully golden and puffy. Remove from the oven and allow the tart to sit on the pan for 5 minutes. Lay a piece of parchment paper on top, followed by a cutting board or plate, and carefully flip the pie over. Peel off the backing paper before serving.

**Sharing is Caring**

# Chicken Parm Pie

Chicken parmigiana is one of those classic Italian-American dishes that I always want to order in a restaurant, but feel that I should go for something a little more contemporary. Yet, it's a classic for a reason—it tastes amazing! The chicken is coated in golden, crisp breadcrumbs, slathered in tomato sauce, and showered in a generous layer of Parmesan cheese. I've taken those key elements and deconstructed them into layers, using some wonderfully tender leftover roast chicken.

## Serves 4–6

2 premade 9¾ x 10½ in sheets of puff pastry or use homemade (see p.12) rolled to 14 x 9 in (35 x 23 cm)
2½oz (75g) slightly stale bread, such as sourdough
3½oz (100g) Parmesan, finely grated, divided
1 tbsp Italian seasoning, divided
drizzle of extra-virgin olive oil
salt and freshly ground black pepper
5 tbsp Slow-Cooked Tomato Sauce (see p.16), or use premade
1 cooked chicken breast, about ⅓lb (150g), shredded, (leftover rotisserie or roast chicken is excellent here)
1 egg, beaten

### YOU WILL NEED
large sheet pan, roughly 15 x 10½ in (38 x 27 cm), lined with parchment paper

1  Preheat the oven to 425°F (220°C). Remove the pastry from the fridge and set aside.

2  In a food processor, blitz the bread with half of the Parmesan and half of the Italian seasoning until you have fine crumbs.

3  Mark out a 14 x 9 in (35 x 23 cm) rectangle on the parchment paper and place it drawn side down on the sheet pan. Drizzle on a liberal amount of olive oil, then sprinkle with the remaining Italian seasoning. Season with salt and pepper.

4  Leaving a ½-in (1-cm) border, sprinkle half of the breadcrumb mixture on the rectangle, followed by dollops of the tomato sauce, then add a layer of the shredded chicken. Follow this with the remaining Parmesan and the rest of the breadcrumbs.

5  Carefully drape the puff pastry over the chicken and breadcrumb mixture. Using the back of a fork, press indentations around the edge of the pastry to seal. Score the top in a diamond pattern with a sharp knife and then brush with egg.

6  Bake for 35–40 minutes, until the pastry is wonderfully golden and puffy. Remove from the oven and allow the tart to sit on the pan for 5 minutes. Lay a piece of parchment paper on top, followed by a cutting board or plate, and carefully flip the pie over. Peel off the backing paper to serve.

**Sharing is Caring**

# Zucchini & Ricotta Phyllo Tart

If you've ever grown your own zucchini, you'll know that just a couple of plants can produce a very generous yield. I'm always on the lookout for recipes to use them up, and this one is wonderful, plus you can get creative with the decoration. My advice would be to cut some paper into strips to try the weave technique first—before you attempt the real thing with zucchini.

## Serves 6

drizzle of extra-virgin olive oil
1 sprig of lemon thyme, leaves picked (regular thyme is also lovely), divided
finely grated zest of 1 unwaxed lemon, divided
salt and freshly ground black pepper
2 zucchini, thinly sliced into ribbons with a vegetable peeler
7oz (200g) ricotta
12 sheets premade phyllo dough, roughly 14 x 9 in (35 x 23 cm)
6 tbsp (100g) butter, melted

**YOU WILL NEED**
large sheet pan, roughly 15 x 10½ in (38 x 27 cm), lined with parchment paper

1   Preheat the oven to 425°F (220°C).

2   Mark out a large rectangle on the parchment paper the same size as the pastry and place it drawn side down on the sheet pan. Drizzle on a liberal amount of olive oil, then sprinkle with half of the thyme and lemon zest. Season with salt and pepper.

3   With the short side of the pan facing you, and leaving a 1¼-in (3-cm) border around the edge, place half of the zucchini strips next to each other vertically, starting from the middle of the drawn rectangle. Season with salt and pepper. Weave the remaining strips of zucchini over and under the first layer. Season again.

4   Dollop the ricotta on top, carefully spreading it out to cover the zucchini, then season with more salt, pepper, and the remaining lemon zest.

5   Roll out the sheets of phyllo, keeping them in a pile. Brush the top sheet with melted butter and lay it, butter side up, over the ricotta and zucchini. Repeat with all the phyllo sheets, brushing with more butter as you go, then scrunch the edges to form a rim around the zucchini lattice. Brush the top of the pastry with more butter.

6   Bake for 30 minutes, or until gloriously golden and crisp on top. Remove from the oven and allow the tart to sit on the pan for 5 minutes. Lay a piece of parchment paper on top, followed by a cutting board or plate, and carefully flip the tart over. Peel off the backing paper. Sprinkle with the remaining thyme before serving.

**Sharing is Caring**

# Cherry Tomato, Nettle, & Mozzarella Phyllo Tart

I love foraging, and where we live in the Lincolnshire Wolds there's an abundance of wonderful edible plants right on our doorstep. One of the most common is the stinging nettle, which has been used as a culinary plant for centuries, with its peppery-sweet flavor similar to arugula. If you're going to pick nettles, the trick is to choose young, tender plants and select the top four leaves. Don't forget to wear gloves, and don't pick from the roadside—for obvious reasons. A quick rinse in boiling water eliminates the sting and the leaves can then be handled without gloves. If you can't bring yourself to use them, spinach, arugula, or basil are equally delicious alternatives.

## Serves 4–6

1 large handful of nettles, use young leaves from the top of the plant (or use arugula, spinach, or basil leaves)
drizzle of extra-virgin olive oil
drizzle of balsamic vinegar
salt and freshly ground black pepper
2 shallots, thinly sliced
5½oz (150g) mix of colorful cherry tomatoes, cut in half
5½oz (150g) mozzarella cheese, drained and torn into pieces
12 sheets premade phyllo dough, roughly 14 x 9in (35 x 23cm)
6 tbsp (100g) butter, melted
1 tbsp chopped chives

### YOU WILL NEED
12in (30cm) deep-sided cast-iron pan (ensure the handle is heat resistant), base-lined with parchment paper

**1** Preheat the oven to 350°F (180°C).

**2** Rinse the nettles in boiling water to eliminate their sting, then drain well and set aside.

**3** Drizzle a little olive oil and balsamic vinegar onto the base of the lined pan. Add half of the nettles, spreading them out evenly, and season with salt and pepper. Next, layer in half of the shallots, tomatoes, and mozzarella, then repeat with a second layer of each, saving a little of the mozzarella to serve.

**4** Roll out the sheets of phyllo, keeping them in a pile. Brush the top sheet of phyllo with butter, then scrunch it up and place on top of the tomatoes in the pan. Brush the next sheet of phyllo with butter, scrunch it, then place on top of the tomatoes, next to the first sheet. Continue until all the phyllo is used and the tomatoes are covered in a layer of scrunched-up phyllo.

**5** Bake for 20 minutes, then turn the oven up to 425°F (220°C) and cook for another 15 minutes, or until the pastry is darkly golden and crisp. Remove from the oven and allow the tart to sit in the pan for 10 minutes. Lay a piece of parchment paper on top, followed by a cutting board or plate and carefully flip the tart out of the pan. Be careful; the pan will be hot so use oven mitts or a kitchen towel. Sprinkle the reserved mozzarella on top and finish with the chives.

**Sharing is Caring**

# Sausage, Mashed Potato, & Gravy Pie

A British classic! This is proper warming comfort food and takes many of us back to childhood mealtimes and chilly winter evenings snuggled in front of the fire. Honestly, nothing could be simpler or tastier than fat, juicy sausages nestled in a pile of smooth, creamy mashed potatoes and drowned in a luscious, rich onion gravy. Yet I've made it even better, if that's possible, by draping it in a cozy blanket of puff pastry.

## Serves 6

2 premade 9¾ x 10½ in sheets of puff pastry or use homemade (see p.12) rolled to 14 x 9 in (35 x 23 cm)
drizzle of extra-virgin olive oil
1 sprig of rosemary, leaves picked
1 sprig of thyme, leaves picked
6 sausages in casings, meat or veggie, each cut into thirds
1½ cups (400g) mashed potatoes (either make your own or buy premade)
1 egg, beaten

### For the onion gravy:
5 tbsp (75g) butter
drizzle of olive oil
1 red onion, cut in half lengthwise and thinly sliced into half rings
pinch of sugar
salt and freshly ground black pepper
1 tbsp chopped rosemary
¾ cup (200ml) red wine, divided
1 tbsp all-purpose flour
2 cups (500ml) vegetable stock

### YOU WILL NEED
large sheet pan, roughly 15 x 10½ in (38 x 27 cm), lined with parchment paper

**Sharing is Caring**

1. Start with the onion gravy. Place a large skillet on medium heat, add the butter and a little olive oil. Add the red onion and a pinch of sugar and sauté for 20 minutes, stirring regularly, until caramelized. Season with salt and pepper and add the rosemary. You need to watch the onions like a hawk so they don't burn or stick, turning down the heat if needed. Stir regularly for another 5 minutes, until golden. Turn the heat up, pour in half of the red wine and stir as it bubbles and evaporates. Stir in the flour, then the vegetable stock and remaining red wine and let it bubble away for 5 minutes. Turn down the heat to its lowest setting and let the gravy gently simmer for at least 10 minutes, until thick and glossy. Set aside.

2. Preheat the oven to 425°F (220°C). Remove the pastry from the fridge and set aside.

3. Mark out a 14 x 9 in (35 x 23 cm) rectangle on the parchment paper and place it drawn side down on the sheet pan. Drizzle on a little olive oil, then sprinkle with the rosemary and thyme. Season with a little salt and pepper.

4. Leaving a ½-in (1-cm) border, sprinkle the chopped sausages in the drawn rectangle, then spoon a little of the gravy over the sausages and into the gaps. Dollop on the mashed potatoes and carefully spread evenly, followed by a few more dollops of the luscious gravy. Save at least one-third of the gravy for serving.

5. Lay the puff pastry over the top of the sausage and mashed potatoes. Using the back of a fork, press indentations around the edge of the pastry to seal. Score the top in a diamond pattern with a sharp knife and then brush with egg.

6. Bake for 30 minutes, or until the pastry is golden and puffy. Remove from the oven and allow the pie to sit on the pan for 5 minutes. Lay a piece of parchment paper on top, followed by a cutting board, and carefully flip it over. Peel off the backing paper. Place the pie back in the oven for a further 5–10 minutes to brown the sausages. Reheat the gravy and pour it over the top of the pie before slicing into portions.

# Burrito Pie

When I was growing up in the UK, Mexican food hadn't really taken off in the way it has now. I had never experienced Mexican food until I visited my friend Shannon, who was studying at a university in Southern California. Her parents took us to a Mexican restaurant that still has to be one of the most stunning meals I've ever eaten. It was utterly mind-blowing. This pie re-creates the memory of that meal ...

## Serves 4–6

1 recipe of homemade pie dough (see p.13) rolled out to roughly 14 x 9 in (35 x 23 cm)
1¼ lb (500g) ground beef
⅔ cup (100g) canned black beans
1 tsp mild chili powder
1 tsp smoked sweet paprika
2 tsp ground cumin
3 tbsp tomato paste
salt and freshly ground black pepper
2 tsp extra-virgin olive oil
2 tsp dried oregano
2 shallots, cut into rings
4 tbsp grated mozzarella cheese, divided
1 (5½oz/150g) pouch of cooked long-grain rice, divided
1 tbsp chili oil
1 egg, beaten

### To serve:
sliced avocado
sour cream
lime wedges
chopped cilantro leaves
fresh red chile, finely sliced

### YOU WILL NEED
large sheet pan, roughly 15 x 10½ in (38 x 27 cm), lined with parchment paper

**1** Preheat the oven to 425°F (220°C). Remove the pastry from the fridge and set aside.

**2** Place the ground beef in a bowl with the black beans, chili powder, smoked paprika, cumin, and tomato paste. Season with salt and pepper and mix well. Set aside.

**3** Mark out a 14 x 9 in (35 x 23 cm) rectangle on the parchment paper and place it drawn side down on the sheet pan. Drizzle on a little olive oil and sprinkle with the oregano. Season with salt and pepper.

**4** Leaving a ½-in (1-cm) border, sprinkle the shallots over the top of the rectangle, followed by a quarter of the grated mozzarella. Top with one-third of the beef mixture, a third of the cooked rice, and another tablespoon of the mozzarella. Continue to layer in this way until all the meat, rice, and mozzarella has been used.

**5** Lay out the puff pastry and drizzle one side with a little chili oil, leaving a narrow border all the way around. Lay the pastry, oil-side down, over the meat mixture. Using the back of a fork, press indentations around the edge of the pastry to seal. Score the top in a diamond pattern with a sharp knife and then brush with egg.

**6** Bake for 35–40 minutes, until wonderfully golden and crisp. Remove from the oven and allow the pie to sit on the pan for 5 minutes, then lay a piece of parchment paper on top, followed by a cutting board, and carefully flip it over. Peel off the backing paper. Dress the top with slices of avocado, dollops of sour cream, a squeeze of lime, and a sprinkling of cilantro and chile.

**Sharing is Caring**

# Upside Down Spanakopita

At 17, I went to Greece with my best friend, Andreas. Our itinerary was to go island hopping and basically drink ourselves into oblivion while soaking up the local culture. But first we had to make a pit-stop and visit Andreas's grandparents in Athens. To be honest, I wasn't looking forward to it, but it turned out to be the best part of the trip. It opened my eyes to authentic Greek cuisine and especially the little crunchy spinach- and cheese-filled phyllo triangles, known as *spanakopita*, you could pick up from the street food vendors. This is my version ...

**Serves 6**

2 tbsp extra-virgin olive oil,
   plus extra for drizzling
handful of dill, chopped, divided
handful of mint, leaves
   chopped, divided
salt and freshly ground
   black pepper
10oz (300g) feta, crumbled,
   divided
2 shallots, thinly sliced
2 large eggs, beaten
3½oz (100g) Greek hard
   cheese, such as kefalotyri
   (or Parmesan), grated
10oz (300g) baby spinach leaves
10 tbsp (150g) butter
12 sheets premade phyllo
   dough, roughly 14 x 9 in
   (35 x 23 cm)

**YOU WILL NEED**
large sheet pan, roughly
   15 x 10½ in (38 x 27 cm),
   lined with parchment paper

**1** Preheat the oven to 425°F (220°C).

**2** Mark out a 14 x 9 in (35 x 23 cm) rectangle on the parchment paper and place it drawn side down on the sheet pan. Drizzle on a little olive oil, then sprinkle with one-third of the dill and mint. Season with salt and pepper.

**3** Leaving a ½-in (1-cm) border, sprinkle a third of the crumbled feta on the rectangle, followed by the shallots.

**4** In a bowl, beat the eggs with the remaining feta, the hard cheese, and the rest of the herbs, then mix well.

**5** Lay one-third of the spinach on top of the shallots, creating a sturdy pile in the middle of the lined sheet pan with a generous 1½-in (4-cm) border around the edge. Spoon on half of the egg mixture, then lay another third of the spinach on top, followed by the remaining egg mixture. Finish with the rest of the spinach and gently press it all down.

**6** Melt the butter in a small pan and mix in the 2 tablespoons of olive oil. Unroll the sheets of phyllo, keeping them in a pile. Brush the top sheet of phyllo with butter and lay it, butter-side up, over the spinach mixture. Continue until you've used all the phyllo sheets. Scrunch the edges of the pie all the way around and brush the top with more butter.

**7** Bake for 35–40 minutes, or until darkly golden and crisp. Remove from the oven and allow the pie to sit on the pan for 5 minutes, then lay a piece of parchment paper on top, followed by a cutting board, and carefully flip it over. Peel off the backing paper and cut the pie into triangles to serve.

**Sharing is Caring**

# Fish & Chips Pie

This pie is the ultimate nostalgia trip for me, back to my favorite meal as a kid. We would come home hungry from school and have our dinner early, and it was often something easy that Mum could throw in the oven. Fish sticks, fries, and peas were a favorite, always with lots of ketchup. I'm going a little fancy here with a homemade tomato sauce, a fancy pea and mint purée, and steak fries. I think it has all the makings of a classic pie that the whole family would be happy to devour come dinnertime.

## Serves 4–6

2 premade 9¾ x 10½ in sheets of puff pastry or use homemade (see p.12) rolled to 14 x 9 in (35 x 23 cm)
extra-virgin olive oil, for drizzling
salt and freshly ground black pepper
8 fish sticks, each cut into 3
5 tbsp Slow-Cooked Tomato Sauce (see p.16), or use premade
5½oz (150g) cooked steak fries
1 egg, beaten
1 recipe quantity of Tartar Sauce (see p.17), to serve
few fronds of dill, to finish

### For the pea purée:
2 cups (300g) frozen peas
½ cup (100g) cottage cheese
juice and finely grated zest of ½ unwaxed lemon
few mint leaves
extra-virgin olive oil, for drizzling

### YOU WILL NEED
large sheet pan, roughly 15 x 10½ in (38 x 27 cm), lined with parchment paper

**1** Preheat the oven to 425°F (220°C). Remove the pastry from the fridge and set aside.

**2** Start by making the pea purée. Cook the peas in boiling water following the instructions on the package until tender. Drain well and allow them to cool slightly. Add the peas to a food processor with the cottage cheese, lemon juice and zest, mint, and a drizzle of olive oil. Whiz to a coarse purée and set aside.

**3** Mark out a 14 x 9 in (35 x 23 cm) rectangle on the parchment paper and place it drawn side down on the sheet pan. Drizzle on a liberal amount of olive oil, then season with salt and pepper.

**4** Leaving a ½-in (1-cm) border, randomly lay the fish sticks on the rectangle. Dot a few spoonfuls of the pea purée and the tomato sauce around the fish sticks, then add the steak fries and the remaining tomato sauce and pea purée. Season with salt and pepper.

**5** Carefully drape the puff pastry over the fillings. Using the back of a fork, press indentations around the edge of the pastry to seal. Score the top in a diamond pattern with a sharp knife and then brush with egg.

**6** Bake for 35–40 minutes, or until the pastry is wonderfully golden and puffy. Remove from the oven and allow the pie to sit on the pan for 5 minutes. Lay a piece of parchment paper on top, followed by a cutting board, and carefully flip the pie over. Peel off the backing paper. Drizzle the tartar sauce on the pie and sprinkle with dill before serving, and enjoy!

**Sharing is Caring**

# Special Occasions

Being a nice Jewish boy from North London, I am absolutely crazy for Christmas. I guess it's because we didn't really celebrate it in a big way growing up that I've now embraced it so deeply. Sure, we would gather for a big family meal on the day, but there was never a tree or any decorations. When I finally had a home of my own I decided to go big on not just Christmas but all the special occasions in our lives. We carve pumpkins and dress up for Halloween, we throw Valentine's parties for everyone we love—there are decorations and cocktails galore and, of course, there's always an abundance of food. We may not have had Christmas at home, but Mum knew how to host a party, and if she taught me anything it's to over-cater for every occasion—it can always go in the freezer! In this chapter, I share my favorite sweet and savory special occasion treats for any event throughout the year, be it Mother's Day, St. Patrick's Day, or New Year's Eve—all with my simple upside-down twist, of course.

# Leftover Christmas Pie

The day after Christmas Day (Boxing Day in the UK), there are three guarantees in our home: there is always an abundance of leftovers; there's always a sheet of premade puff pastry in the fridge; and it's a fact that we won't be moving from our armchairs for the whole day. That's why this pie is just so genius. It's the easiest thing to cobble together, yet it tastes like the fanciest thing you've ever made. Obviously, this would work just as well as a leftover Thanksgiving pie, so knock yourself out! I've used the leftovers we usually have in our house, but anything would work here, so go for whatever you've got left. Time to be creative ...

### Serves 4–6

2 premade 9¾ x 10½ in sheets of puff pastry or use homemade (see p.12) rolled to 14 x 9 in (35 x 23 cm)
drizzle of extra-virgin olive oil
2 sprigs of rosemary, leaves picked
2 sprigs of thyme, leaves picked
salt and freshly ground black pepper
½ lb (200g) mixed leftover roasted veggies, such as carrots, potatoes, and Brussels sprouts, cut in half or batons as needed
roughly 4 tbsp leftover stuffing
roughly 4 tbsp leftover mashed potatoes
4–5 slices of leftover ham or bacon
5–6 slices of leftover roast turkey
4 tsp cranberry sauce
1 egg, beaten

### YOU WILL NEED
large sheet pan, roughly 15 x 10½ in (38 x 27 cm), lined with parchment paper

1 Preheat the oven to 425°F (220°C). Remove the pastry from the fridge and set aside.

2 Mark out a 14 x 9 in (35 x 23 cm) rectangle on the parchment paper and place it drawn side down on the sheet pan. Drizzle on a little olive oil, then sprinkle with the rosemary and thyme. Season with salt and pepper.

3 Leaving a ½-in (1-cm) border, layer the leftover veggies in the rectangle, followed by the stuffing, mashed potatoes, and rolled up slices of ham or bacon, and then tuck the turkey into any crevices you can find! Dollop spoonfuls of cranberry sauce all over and then season the top with salt and pepper.

4 Lay the puff pastry over the top of the leftover mixture. Using the back of a fork, press indentations around the edge of the pastry to seal. Score the top in a diamond pattern with a sharp knife and then brush with egg.

5 Bake for 35 minutes, or until the pastry is wonderfully golden and puffy. Remove from the oven and allow the pie to sit on the pan for 5 minutes. Lay a piece of parchment paper on top, followed by a cutting board, and carefully flip the pie over. Peel off the backing paper. You may want to slide the tart back onto the sheet pan and into the oven for a few minutes to get a little more golden on top before serving.

**Special Occasions**

# Chili Shrimp, Honey, & Bacon Canapés

When we were kids, Mum and Dad came back from a trip to California with a new dish for the grill: shrimp wrapped in bacon on a skewer. It may sound simple to our 21st-century ears but back in my youth our minds were blown; the sticky, salty sweetness combined into one divine mouthful was phenomenal. I've added an upside-down version to my list of party canapés for pure nostalgia.

## Makes 12

2 premade 9¾ x 10½ in sheets
   of puff pastry or use
   homemade (see p.12) rolled
   to 14 x 9 in (35 x 23 cm)
drizzle of extra-virgin olive oil
drizzle of honey
1 tsp dried chili flakes
handful of dill, roughly chopped
3½oz (100g) bacon, cut into
   small pieces
12 large raw peeled shrimp
   (frozen works well), deveined
⅓ cup (100g) ketchup, or
   Slow-Cooked Tomato Sauce
   (see p.16)
1 tbsp sriracha
1 large egg, beaten
squeeze of lime juice, to finish

### YOU WILL NEED

large sheet pan, roughly
   15 x 10½ in (38 x 27 cm),
   lined with parchment paper
2¾-in (7-cm) round cookie
   cutter, ramekin, or bowl

1  Preheat the oven to 375°F (190°C). Remove the pastry from the fridge and set aside.

2  Drizzle a little olive oil on the lined sheet pan, placed horizontally in front of you, followed by a drizzle of honey, then sprinkle with the chili flakes and dill.

3  Arrange 3–4 pieces of chopped bacon per tart on the seasoned oil. Place a shrimp on top of each pile of bacon.

4  Lay out the puff pastry and use the cookie cutter, ramekin, or bowl to cut out 12 small disks. Mix the ketchup and sriracha together in a small bowl, and spread a teaspoon of the mixture over each disk, leaving a narrow border around the edge

5  Lay the pastry, sauce-side down, over the shrimp and bacon. Using the back of a fork, press indentations around the edge of each disk to seal. Score the top in a diamond pattern with a sharp knife and then brush with egg.

6  Bake for 10 minutes, then turn the oven down to 375°F (190°C) and cook for a further 15–20 minutes, until golden and puffy. Remove from the oven and let the canapés sit on the pan for 5 minutes before flipping them over with a spatula. Add a squeeze of lime before serving.

**Special Occasions**

# New Year's Eve Ham & Stilton Canapés

By the time New Year's Eve rolls around I'm pretty much done with rich Christmas food, but for some reason there's always a little Stilton and Christmas ham left in the fridge. These cute little upside-down canapés use up any leftovers and are perfect for any Hogmanay hoopla or New Year's Eve party you may be throwing.

**Makes 12**

2 premade 9¾ x 10½ in sheets of puff pastry or use homemade (see p.12) rolled to 14 x 9 in (35 x 23 cm)
drizzle of extra-virgin olive oil
2 sprigs of thyme, leaves picked
salt and freshly ground black pepper
3½oz (100g) Stilton cheese, crumbled
few thick slices of Christmas ham, torn into 12 bite-size pieces
3 tbsp Christmas chutney or caramelized onion jam
1 egg, beaten
few chives, snipped, to finish

**YOU WILL NEED**

large sheet pan, roughly 15 x 10½ in (38 x 27 cm), lined with parchment paper

**1** Preheat the oven to 400°F (200°C). Remove the pastry from the fridge and set aside.

**2** Drizzle a little olive oil on the lined sheet pan, placed horizontally in front of you, then sprinkle with thyme and season with salt and pepper.

**3** Place the crumbled Stilton on the seasoned oil. I use a few pieces of Stilton per tart. Use a piece of ham per tart and place them on top of the Stilton, then add a small dollop of chutney or jam to each pile.

**4** Lay out the puff pastry and cut into 12 small bite-size pieces. Place a piece of pastry over each pile of Stilton, ham, and chutney or jam.

**5** Using the back of a fork, press indentations around the edge of each canapé to seal. Score a cross diagonally over the top with a sharp knife and then brush with egg.

**6** Bake for 10 minutes, then turn the oven down to 375°F (190°C) and cook for a further 20 minutes, until wonderfully golden and puffy. Remove from the oven and let the tarts sit on the pan for 5 minutes before flipping them over with a spatula. Sprinkle with the chives before serving.

**Special Occasions**

# Garlic, Mushroom, & Rosemary "Vol au Vents"

These fabulous little puffs of joy are a classic for a reason and worthy of a comeback in my humble opinion. What I love about these canapés is just how quick and easy they are to throw together, yet they look super fancy. I love the idea of serving them upside down at a party and then allowing your guests to pick one up and flip it over before eating. Make sure you loosen them on the sheet pan first.

**Makes 12**

2 premade 9¾ x 10½ in sheets of puff pastry or use homemade (see p.12) rolled to 14 x 9 in (35 x 23 cm)
drizzle of extra-virgin olive oil
1 sprig of rosemary, leaves picked
salt and freshly ground black pepper
12 shiitake mushrooms, stalks trimmed
1 garlic clove, peeled and cut into 12 slivers
2½oz (75g) Parmesan, finely grated
3½oz (100g) cream cheese
1 large egg, beaten

**YOU WILL NEED**
large sheet pan, roughly 15 x 10½ in (38 x 27 cm), lined with parchment paper

1   Preheat the oven to 425°F (220°C). Remove the pastry from the fridge and set aside.

2   Drizzle a little olive oil on the lined sheet pan, placed horizontally in front of you, sprinkle with the rosemary, then season with salt and pepper

3   Arrange the mushrooms on the seasoned oil. I use 1 mushroom per canapé (you can cut them in half if they are on the large side). Place a sliver of garlic on top of each mushroom and then sprinkle with the Parmesan.

4   Lay out the puff pastry and cut it into 12 small bite-size pieces. Spread a teaspoon of cream cheese over each piece, leaving a narrow border around the edge.

5   Lay a piece of pastry, cream cheese side down, over each mushroom. Using the back of a fork, press indentations around the edge of each canapé to seal. Score the top in a diamond pattern with a sharp knife and then brush with egg.

6   Bake for 25 minutes, or until wonderfully golden and puffy. Remove from the oven and allow the canapés to sit on the pan for 5 minutes before flipping them over. Test that they're loose first and you should be able to pick them up by hand and flip them right side up.

**Special Occasions**

# Burns Night Cullen Skink Canapés

I absolutely adore Scotland, the people (the first boy I kissed was Scottish, and that accent, oh my!), the majestic landscape, and, naturally, the wonderful food, from the traditional to the modern. It's a place filled with joy and wonder, not least when it's time for a celebration. The Scots really know how to party! I'm celebrating Scotland's national poet, Robbie Burns, with these canapés, and while Cullen skink, which is a thick Scottish soup made of smoked haddock, potatoes, and onions, isn't traditionally eaten on Burns Night, it is my favorite traditional Scottish dish and works perfectly here.

## Makes 12

2 premade 9¾ x 10½ in sheets of puff pastry or use homemade (see p.12) rolled to 14 x 9 in (35 x 23 cm)
drizzle of olive oil
2 skinless smoked haddock fillets, cut into 12 chunks
⅔ cup (150g) Cheesy Sauce (see p.54)
3½ oz (100g) strong Scottish Cheddar cheese
1 cup (150g) mashed potatoes (I use premade)
1 large egg, beaten
few chives, snipped, to finish

### For the caramelized onion:
2 tbsp (30g) butter
drizzle of extra-virgin olive oil
1 large onion, thinly sliced
salt and freshly ground black pepper
½ tsp sugar
2 tbsp Scottish whisky

### YOU WILL NEED
large sheet pan, roughly 15 x 10½ in (38 x 27 cm), lined with parchment paper

**1** Start by making the caramelized onion. Heat a skillet on medium heat and add the pat of butter and a drizzle of olive oil. Add the onion, season with salt and pepper and sauté gently, stirring often, for about 10 minutes, until soft and translucent. Turn up the heat to medium-high, add the sugar and cook the onion, stirring often, for another 20 minutes, until darkly golden. Pour in the whisky and let it bubble away. When all the liquid is absorbed, take the pan off the heat and set aside to cool slightly.

**2** Preheat the oven to 425°F (220°C). Remove the pastry from the fridge and set aside.

**3** Drizzle a little olive oil over the lined sheet pan, placed horizontally in front of you, then season with salt and pepper. Arrange the pieces of smoked haddock over the seasoned oil. I use 1 piece of fish per canapé and place them 4 rows across by 3 rows down. Place a teaspoon of the caramelized onion on top of each piece of fish, followed by a dollop of the thick cheese sauce.

**4** In a bowl, mix the Cheddar into the mashed potatoes until well combined. Set aside.

**5** Lay out the puff pastry and cut into 12 small bite-size pieces. Spread a generous teaspoon of the Cheddar potatoes over each one, leaving a narrow border around the edge. Lay the pastry, potato side down, over the haddock mixture. Using the back of a fork, press indentations around the edge of each canapé to seal. Score the top in a diamond pattern with a sharp knife and then brush with egg.

**6** Bake for 25 minutes, or until gloriously golden. Remove from the oven and let the canapés sit on the pan for 5 minutes before flipping them over with a spatula. Sprinkle with the chives.

**Special Occasions**

# Chocolate & Berry Valentine's Heart Tart

I pretend not to be, but I'm a big old softy. A true romantic at heart. I love to give gifts to my loved ones, especially in food form. They say the secret to someone's heart is through their stomach, but for me it's about the joy and love they show on their faces when they bite into that yummy chocolate tart.

## Serves 2–4

2 premade 9¾ x 10½ in sheets of puff pastry or use homemade (see p.12) rolled to 14 x 9 in (35 x 23 cm)
drizzle of honey
2 tbsp mini candy hearts, plus extra to decorate
2 tbsp freeze-dried raspberries
6–8 strawberries, hulled and cut in half from root to tip
5 maraschino cherries, cut in half
2 tbsp mini pink and white marshmallows, plus extra to decorate
2 tbsp chocolate hazelnut spread
1 egg, beaten
powdered sugar, for dusting

### YOU WILL NEED
large sheet pan, roughly 15 x 10½ in (38 x 27 cm), lined with parchment paper

1   Preheat the oven to 425°F (220°C). Remove the pastry from the fridge and set aside.

2   Cut out a large heart shape on a piece of thin cardboard to use as a template. Ensure it fits on your sheet pan and is no bigger than the sheet of puff pastry. Lay the heart shape onto the sheet of parchment paper and draw around it, then turn the sheet over and place it, drawn side down, on the sheet pan. You can make a few smaller hearts, too, if you have room on the sheet pan and to use up any remaining pastry, or save the leftovers for another recipe (see pp.14–15).

3   Leaving a ½-in (1-cm) border, drizzle a little honey over the heart, then sprinkle with the candy hearts and freeze-dried raspberries. Lay the strawberry halves on top, followed by the cherries. I prefer a relaxed arrangement, but feel free to create a pattern with your fruit. Sprinkle with the marshmallows and then drizzle with chocolate spread.

4   Roll out the puff pastry and, using the same heart template as before, cut around it and lay the pastry over the top of the fruit mixture. Using a spoon, press around the edge of the pastry heart to seal. Score the top in a diamond pattern with a sharp knife and then brush with egg.

5   Bake for 35 minutes, or until the pastry is wonderfully golden and puffy. Remove from the oven and allow the tart to sit on the pan for 5 minutes. Lay a piece of parchment paper on top, followed by a cutting board or plate, and carefully flip the tart over. Peel off the backing paper. Sprinkle the top with extra marshmallows and candy hearts and dust with a little powdered sugar.

Special Occasions

# St. Patrick's Day Bacon & Colcannon Pie

I've drunk in many a bar around the world but never been quite as merry as I was in Dublin. There's something about the city and the people that just makes merriment all the merrier! After speaking with a few close Irish friends, it turns out there isn't a traditional Irish dish that's specifically eaten on the day, so I've gone with an absolute classic, colcannon—a mix of creamy mashed potatoes with cabbage and bacon—for my upside-down pie.

### Serves 4–6

2 premade 9¾ x 10½ in sheets of puff pastry or use homemade (see p.12) rolled to 14 x 9 in (35 x 23 cm)
½ small Napa cabbage, roughly chopped
½ cup (120ml) whole milk
½ vegetable bouillon cube
5 tbsp (80g) butter, divided
3 tbsp (25g) all-purpose flour
2 tbsp whole grain mustard
salt and freshly ground black pepper
1¼ cups (200g) mashed potatoes (I always use premade)
drizzle of extra-virgin olive oil
1 sprig of rosemary, leaves picked
1 sprig of thyme, leaves picked
5 slices of thick-cut bacon, chopped
1 egg, beaten

### YOU WILL NEED

large sheet pan, roughly 15 x 10½ in (38 x 27 cm), lined with parchment paper

1  Preheat the oven to 425°F (220°C). Remove the pastry from the fridge and set aside.

2  In a saucepan, add the cabbage and milk with ½ cup (120ml) of water. Bring to a boil, crumble in the bouillon cube and cook the cabbage for 4 minutes, until just tender. Strain the cabbage, saving the stock, and set aside. Return the stock to the pan. Add the 3 tbsp (50g) butter and the flour and stir with a balloon whisk for about 3 minutes, until thickened. Stir in the mustard and season with salt and pepper. Set aside to cool slightly.

3  In a large bowl, mix the mashed potatoes and cooked cabbage with a little salt and pepper and the remaining 2 tbsp (30g) butter. Set aside.

4  Mark out a 14 x 9 in (35 x 23 cm) rectangle on the parchment paper and place it drawn side down on the sheet pan. Drizzle on a little olive oil, then sprinkle with the rosemary and thyme. Season with salt and pepper.

5  Leaving a ½-in (1-cm) border, dot half of the bacon over the rectangle and then add half of the potato and cabbage mixture. Carefully, pour on ½ cup (100ml) of the thick cabbage gravy. You don't want the mixture to be too wet, just enough to add a little lubrication. Add the remaining bacon pieces and spoonfuls of cabbage mixture. Pour a bit more gravy on top.

6  Lay the puff pastry over the cabbage mixture. Using the back of a fork, press indentations around the edge of the pastry to seal. Score the top in a diamond pattern with a sharp knife and then brush with egg.

7  Bake for 35 minutes, or until the pastry is golden and puffy. Remove from the oven and allow the pie to sit on the pan for 5 minutes. Lay a piece of parchment paper on top, followed by a cutting board, and carefully flip the pie over. Peel off the backing paper. Slide the pie back onto the sheet pan and into the oven for a few minutes to get a little more golden on top.

**Special Occasions**

# Mother's Day Shrimp & Pommes Frites Tarts

Mother's Day is very special for lots of people, but I always find it tricky knowing exactly what to get my mum (not that she's picky obviously ... ahem). So I sent her a message asking if she could eat anything in the world for Mother's Day, what would it be? Her answer was shrimp with garlic butter and pommes frites! Proof that you can take the "fish and chips" girl out of Hull but you can never truly take Hull out of the girl. This one's for you, Mum. X

## Makes 2 (1 for me and 1 for Mum!)

2 premade 9¾ x 10½ in sheets of puff pastry or use homemade (see p.12) rolled to 14 x 9 in (35 x 23 cm)
½lb (200g) frozen raw jumbo shrimp, peeled and deveined (roughly 12 shrimp)
7oz (200g) precooked pommes frites (these could be frozen or takeout French fries), left to cool
1 egg, beaten
few chives, snipped, to finish

### For the garlic butter:
10 tbsp (150g) butter, softened
3 garlic cloves, finely chopped
1 sprig of rosemary, leaves picked and finely chopped
1 sprig of thyme, leaves picked and finely chopped
salt and freshly ground black pepper

### YOU WILL NEED
large sheet pan, roughly 15 x 10½ in (38 x 27 cm), lined with parchment paper

1   Preheat the oven to 425°F (220°C). Remove the pastry from the fridge and set aside.

2   First make the garlic butter. Place the softened butter in a bowl and mix in the garlic and herbs, then season with salt and pepper until combined. Set aside.

3   Mark out 2 large rectangles on the sheet of parchment paper, roughly 6½ x 9 in (17 x 23 cm), leaving space between each one. Place the parchment paper back on the pan, drawn side down.

4   Leaving a ½-in (1-cm) border, slather 2 tablespoons of the garlic butter over each rectangle. Lay the shrimp in 2 piles on the garlic butter—you can do this in neat little rows or randomly, it doesn't matter. I use roughly 6 shrimp per tart. Spoon a few teaspoons of the garlic butter over the shrimp and top with the pommes frites in a pile. You should be quite generous here. Spoon the remaining garlic butter on top of the pommes frites.

5   Lay out the puff pastry and cut it into 2 rectangles the same size as those drawn on the parchment paper. Lay the pastry rectangles over the seafood and frites. Using the back of a fork, press indentations around the edges of the pastry to seal. Score the top in a diamond pattern with a sharp knife and then brush with egg

6   Bake for 25 minutes, or until the pastry is gloriously golden. Remove from the oven and allow the tarts to sit on the pan for 5 minutes. Lay a piece of parchment paper on top, followed by a cutting board or plate and carefully flip the tarts over. Peel off the backing paper before serving sprinkled with chives.

**Special Occasions**

# Halloween Sausage & Cranberry "Mummy" Heads

I simply love Halloween. There's a wonderful community spirit to it. I guess it's something about the celebration of witches and all things spooky that brings us weirdos together, as well as an excuse to dress up, of course. These upside-down mummy heads are pure silliness. I'm using pastry off-cuts for the bandages and little stuffed peppers and olives for the eyes. Sausage mixed with cranberry jelly make the zombie flesh. In my humble opinion, they're spooktacular!

## Makes 4

2 premade 9¾ x 10½ in sheets
   of puff pastry or use
   homemade (see p.12) rolled
   to 14 x 9 in (35 x 23 cm)
4 pork or veggie sausages
2 tsp cranberry jelly
4 black pitted olives, cut
   in half
4 ricotta-stuffed baby peppers,
   cut in half
drizzle of extra-virgin olive oil
salt and freshly ground
   black pepper
1 egg, beaten

### YOU WILL NEED
large sheet pan, roughly
   15 x 10½ in (38 x 27 cm),
   lined with parchment paper

1 Preheat the oven to 425°F (220°C). Remove the pastry from the fridge and set aside.

2 Place your sausages in a bowl and mash them a little with a fork. Add the cranberry jelly and lightly mix—you want bits of red oozing through. Set aside. Press half an olive into each stuffed pepper half so it looks like an eyeball. Repeat to make 8 eyeballs in total, then set aside.

3 Mark out 4 rectangles on the sheet of parchment paper, roughly 4 x 5½ in (10 x 14 cm), leaving space between each one. Place the parchment paper back on the pans, drawn side down. Drizzle a little olive oil on each rectangle and season with salt and pepper.

4 Roll out the pastry, place it horizontally on the worktop and cut off six ½-in (1-cm) wide strips from one side for the bandages.

5 With the sheet pan placed vertically, arrange three of the pastry strips across two of the rectangles. Think of the rectangle like a face covered in bandages, and place 2 eyeballs, with the olive-side facing downward, toward the top of a rectangle. Repeat to make three more faces.

6 Cut the remaining pastry into quarters, about the same size as those drawn on the parchment paper. Leaving a ½-in (1-cm) border, slather one side of each rectangle with the sausage mixture. Lay the pastry rectangles, sausage side down, over the bandages. Trim any excess pastry from the bandages. Using the back of a fork, press indentations around the edge of the pastry to seal. Score the top of each one in a diamond pattern with a sharp knife and then brush with egg.

7 Bake for 35 minutes, until the pastry is golden and puffy. Remove from the oven and let the tarts sit on the pan for 5 minutes before flipping them over with a spatula.

**Special Occasions**

# Smoked Salmon & Cream Cheese Canapés

Growing up, if we were having family over for an event, Mum would usually lay on some kind of buffet, and smoked salmon and cream cheese bagels were always on the table. I think it partly goes back to our Jewish roots, but also to the fact that smoked salmon was a luxury when I was young. It felt very fancy tucking into ribbons of the delicately smoked fish. That's why I created these gorgeous little party canapés. They work for any kind of party, and can be frozen, uncooked, on the sheet pans and then placed directly into the hot oven from frozen, simply increasing the cooking time by 5 minutes.

## Makes 24

4 premade 9¾ x 10½ in sheets of puff pastry or use 2 batches homemade (see p.12) each rolled to 14 x 9 in (35 x 23 cm)
drizzle of extra-virgin olive oil
handful of dill, chopped, plus extra to serve
salt and freshly ground black pepper
3½oz (100g) smoked salmon, sliced into 24 bite-size pieces
1 (8oz/250g) package cream cheese
1 large egg, beaten
squeeze of lemon juice, to finish

### YOU WILL NEED
2 large sheet pans, roughly 15 x 10½ in (38 x 27 cm), lined with parchment paper

1 Preheat the oven to 400°F (200°C). Remove the pastry from the fridge and set aside.

2 Drizzle a little olive oil on the lined sheet pans, placed horizontally in front of you, sprinkle with dill, then season with salt and pepper.

3 Arrange slices of smoked salmon over the seasoned oil, evenly spacing them out. I use 1 piece of salmon per tart. Dollop a spoonful of cream cheese on top of each piece of salmon.

4 Lay out the puff pastry and cut each sheet into 12 small bite-size pieces. Lay a piece of pastry over each piece of salmon and cream cheese.

5 Using the back of a fork, press indentations around the edge of each canapé to seal. Score a cross diagonally over the top with a sharp knife and then brush with egg.

6 Bake for 10 minutes, then turn the oven down to 375°F (190°C) and cook for a further 15–20 minutes, until golden and puffy. Remove from the oven and let the tarts sit on the pans for 5 minutes before flipping them over with a spatula. A squeeze of lemon juice and a sprig of dill before serving gives them an extra lift!

**Special Occasions**

# Soups, Salads & Sides

When asked what she served with her famous 24-hour roast beef, my Auntie Jeannie would always say "whatever carb you like." It's a great answer because it took the onus away from her and also meant the person cooking got to choose their favorite side dish. I guess I get a little bit of my "eat whatever you fancy" attitude from her. I've never been one for creating or planning the perfect complete meal. One could call it pure luck (or poor planning) that I can open the fridge, pull out a few odd items and knock something together. I love the challenge, so I always find it slightly amusing when people ask me what they should serve with a certain dish. I want to say "whatever's in the fridge," à la Auntie Jeannie, but I guess that doesn't work for everyone. So here's a collection of my favorite dishes to eat with my upside-down tarts and pies. I wouldn't necessarily call them all side dishes, but they are wonderful accompaniments to many of the recipes featured in this book.

# Potato, Carrot, & Onion Kugel

This is a traditional eastern European Jewish dish, originally served during festivals. It's like a giant rosti and is very simple to make, usually consisting of just grated potato and onion, but I had some carrots to use up and thought they'd make a nice addition. A kugel is a great accompaniment to any meal that calls for carbs as a side dish. Mum serves it in slices in place of roast potatoes with Friday night dinner and, of course, it would work well with the Full English Breakfast Pie (see p.53).

## Serves 4–6

butter, for greasing
5 Russet potatoes, cut into
    large chunks
2 large carrots, cut into
    large chunks
2 large onions, finely grated
2 eggs, beaten
2 tbsp all-purpose flour
large handful of rosemary
    leaves
2 tbsp extra-virgin olive oil
salt and freshly ground
    black pepper

### YOU WILL NEED
8-in (20-cm) loose-bottomed
    fluted tart pan or similarly
    sized cake pan

1  Grease the base and the sides of the fluted tart pan with butter.

2  Par-boil the potatoes and carrots in a large saucepan of boiling water until just beginning to yield, drain, and set aside to cool. Once cool, place in the fridge for 1 hour to chill. I usually cook mine the night before.

3  When ready to make the kugel, preheat the oven to 425°F (220°C). Once the potatoes and carrots are cold, finely grate them into a large bowl. Add the grated onions with the rest of the ingredients and mix together well.

4  Put the mixture into your tart pan, spread it out evenly, and roast in the oven for 40 minutes, or until golden and crisp around the edges. Serve cut into wedges.

# Roasted Tomato & Feta Soup

Sweet and rich from the slow-roasted vegetables, a little bite of heat from the dried chili flakes, and rounded off beautifully with the salty tang of feta cheese, this is a bowl of comfort—the soup equivalent of a hug. It is literally perfection in soup form, plus the wonderful orange color is bound to brighten up even the gloomiest of days. I think it would pair perfectly with any of the cheesy tarts in the book, such as the Shallot & Cream Cheese Tarts (see p.20) or the Cheesy Potato Tarts (see p.25), taking the classic combination of tomato soup and grilled cheese to another level.

## Serves 4–6

1 (14.5oz/400g) can diced tomatoes
1 red onion, cut into wedges
1 large potato, peeled and chopped into chunks
1 tsp tomato paste
3 whole garlic cloves, peeled
12 small tomatoes on the vine
1 tsp salt
1 tsp freshly ground black pepper
½ tsp dried chili flakes
1 tsp dried oregano
drizzle of extra-virgin olive oil
3 cups (750ml) vegetable stock
dash of white wine (optional)
5½oz (150g) feta, crumbled, divided

**YOU WILL NEED**
large, shallow cast-iron Dutch oven or deep ovenproof dish with lid

1   Preheat the oven to 375°F (190°C).

2   Empty the can of diced tomatoes into the ovenproof dish. Add the onion, potato, tomato paste, and garlic. Lay the vine tomatoes on top (on the vine is fine). Season with the salt and pepper, chili flakes, and dried oregano, and then drizzle liberally with olive oil.

3   Place the casserole dish in the oven and roast slowly for 30–45 minutes, until the potato is tender and the onion has started to brown. Carefully remove the casserole dish from the oven and pick out the vine from the tomatoes. Pour in the stock and wine (if using), then add 3½oz (100g) of the crumbled feta and stir well.

4   Pop the lid on and place the casserole dish back in the oven for a further 20 minutes. Remove from the oven and let it cool for roughly 15 minutes before blending with an immersion blender. Serve topped with the remaining crumbled feta.

**Soups, Salads, & Sides**

# Chilled Leek, Potato, & Lemongrass Soup

The addition of lemongrass to the classic pairing of leek and potato is wonderful, elevating the taste of this chilled soup to one of summery joy. It would make a perfect accompaniment to the Smoked Salmon & Cream Cheese Canapés (see p.98).

**Serves 4–6**

2 tbsp (30g) butter
drizzle of extra-virgin olive oil
2 shallots, finely chopped
½ fennel bulb. chopped
1 large leek, chopped
2 potatoes, peeled and chopped
2 garlic cloves, grated
1 tsp thyme leaves
salt and freshly ground
    black pepper
6 asparagus stalks, chopped
2 cups (500ml) good-quality
    vegetable stock
2 cups (500ml) milk (any type
    will work—I used skim milk)
2 lemongrass stalks
1 tbsp cream cheese (optional)
chilled cucumber, diced, to
    serve
chopped chives, to serve

1 Heat the butter (leeks love butter) and a drizzle of olive oil in a large saucepan on medium heat. When they begin to sizzle, add the shallots, fennel, leek, and potatoes and sauté for about 8 minutes with some gentle stirring.

2 Add the garlic, thyme, and some salt and pepper. Stir in the asparagus, then pop the lid on and let it all sweat for a further 5 minutes.

3 Pour the stock and milk into the pan. Bend the lemongrass stalks—you don't want them to break into pieces, just snap so they release their fragrance into the soup. Place the lemongrass in the soup, turn down the heat and let it gently simmer for 10 minutes. Check on it frequently because the milk tends to boil over. A quick stir should help it calm down. Turn the heat off, place the lid on, and let the soup cool.

4 Take the lemongrass stalks out and stir in the cream cheese, if using. This isn't 100 percent necessary but it 100 percent should be! Using an immersion blender, blend until velvety smooth and creamy. Pour the soup into a container and pop it in the fridge for at least 3 hours, or until fully chilled. Serve topped with diced cucumber and chopped chives.

**Soups, Salads, & Sides**

# Warm Caprese Salad with Roasted Tomato Vinaigrette

This salad, which is my take on the classic combination of tomato, mozzarella, and basil, is sunshine on a plate, but it's the wonderful (and very simple) dressing that really makes it shine. I slow-roast the tomatoes in olive oil and balsamic vinegar to create a rich vinaigrette that simply oozes with the signature flavors of the Mediterranean. It makes the perfect side salad to the Beet, Red Onion, & Goat Cheese Tart (see p.48).

**Serves 4**

18–20 ripe cherry tomatoes on the vine
2 sprigs of rosemary
large handful of basil, plus extra leaves to serve
4 garlic cloves
3 tbsp extra-virgin olive oil
3 tbsp balsamic vinegar
salt and freshly ground black pepper
1 tsp Dijon mustard
handful of fresh green beans, trimmed
3½oz (100g) arugula
3 large vine-ripened tomatoes, cut into wedges
2 ripe avocados, stones removed, peeled and sliced
7oz (200g) mozzarella cheese, drained and torn into chunks
handful of chopped chives, to serve

**1** Preheat the oven to 400°F (200°C).

**2** Place the cherry tomatoes on their vines in a roasting pan with the rosemary, basil, and garlic. Drizzle with the olive oil and balsamic vinegar, then season with salt and pepper. Roast for 30–40 minutes, until the tomatoes are tender. Remove the tomatoes from the vine (they will burst). Leave 6 tomatoes in the roasting pan and set the others aside.

**3** Add the mustard to the pan and stir well, crushing the tomatoes as you go. This will be the dressing for your salad—it's amazing!

**4** Steam the green beans until tender, then set aside.

**5** Now build the salad on a large platter. I start with a bed of arugula, then layer with the tomato wedges, green beans, avocado, and mozzarella. Spoon the reserved roasted tomatoes on top, then drizzle with the dressing. Serve topped with basil leaves and the chopped chives.

**Soups, Salads, & Sides**

# Chopped Salad with Smoked Chili-Fried Chickpeas

In the summer between lockdowns we ventured to Cornwall. It was a glorious trip after having been shut away safely in our home. I remember walking around with wide-eyed, childlike wonder. It all looked so fresh and amazing and everything we ate tasted like we'd never eaten before! To this day, I remember eating chili-fried chickpeas at The Rocket Store in Boscastle. They were sensational and inspired me to make this salad, which pairs perfectly with the Carrot, Cilantro, & Feta Tarts (see p.41).

**Serves 4**

1 (15.5oz/400g) can chickpeas, drained and rinsed
drizzle of chili oil
½ tsp dried chili flakes
½ tsp smoked sweet paprika
salt and freshly ground black pepper
2 romaine lettuce hearts or salad leaves of your choice, chopped
½ cucumber, quartered and chopped
1 large heirloom beef tomato, chopped into chunky pieces
8 cherry tomatoes, halved
8 olives
5½oz (150g) manchego cheese, cut into cubes
⅔ cup (100g) frozen peas, defrosted
1 avocado, stone removed, peeled and chopped

**For the creamy dressing:**
2½oz (75g) cream cheese
large handful of basil leaves
2 tbsp Greek yogurt
handful of oregano
handful of chives
drizzle of olive oil
juice and finely grated zest of 1 unwaxed lemon

1 Remove the skin from the chickpeas—this may seem like a fiddle and an unnecessary step but it's super quick. You just squeeze the chickpeas out of their skins and it allows them to crisp up much faster in the skillet.

2 Place the chickpeas in a bowl and douse them liberally in chili oil, chili flakes, and smoked paprika. Season with salt and stir well until combined.

3 Heat a large skillet over high heat until nice and hot, then fry the chickpeas for roughly 8 minutes, until crisp, tossing them regularly. Set aside.

4 Place all the ingredients for the creamy dressing into a blender or a bowl and blend or whisk until smooth. Season with salt and pepper.

5 Build your salad as you like using the salad leaves, cucumber, tomatoes, olives, manchego, peas, avocado (I like leaving the veggies nice and chunky for texture), and the fried chickpeas, then pour the dressing over with wild abandon.

**Soups, Salads, & Sides**

# Leftover Veggie Slaw with Mint, Pea, & Cottage Cheese Dressing

This is my favorite kind of meal. Like most of us, I tend to buy a whole bunch of random veggies and then at the end of the week there's always that half a cabbage or some stray carrots that need eating up. This is where a slaw comes in. I adore a slaw that you can throw anything and everything into. And then I finish it with a toss-it-all-in dressing too—here it's cottage cheese, basil, mint, peas, and mayo—to give the salad a boost, and there you have it. It's perfect with the Hawaiian Pizza (see p.60).

## Serves 4

3 tbsp (50g) butter
drizzle of extra-virgin olive oil
1 bunch of asparagus, stalks
   chopped and tips left whole
salt and freshly ground
   black pepper
½ Napa cabbage, finely sliced
1 carrot, finely sliced
½ cauliflower, leaves removed,
   florets roughly chopped
2 celery stalks, finely chopped

### For the dressing:
2 tbsp cottage cheese
1 heaped tbsp torn basil leaves
1 heaped tbsp chopped mint
½ tbsp chopped chives
⅓ cup (50g) frozen peas,
   defrosted
1 tbsp mayonnaise (see p.17),
   or use premade
juice of ½ lemon

1  Heat the butter and a drizzle of olive oil in a skillet on medium heat. Throw in the asparagus, season with salt and pepper, then sauté for 5 minutes. Turn the heat off, cover with the lid, and set aside while you prepare the rest of the veggies.

2  Place the cabbage, carrots, cauliflower, and celery in a large serving bowl and set aside.

3  To make the dressing, place all the ingredients in a pitcher and blitz with an immersion blender until combined.

4  Add the warm asparagus to the bowl of prepared vegetables, pour the dressing in and mix well before serving.

**Note:** I used all the veggies that needed eating up in my fridge. Feel free to add what you love and what needs using up in yours.

**Soups, Salads, & Sides**

# Roasted Potato & Tomato Salad

Every summer, when new potatoes are fresh out of the ground, this is my go-to salad. I always like to add a twist, and this year I'm roasting the potatoes, but what makes this salad even more special is that I'm coating them in a roasted tomato mayonnaise dressing. Believe me, this salad is incredible and I have pretty much served it with everything that came out of the kitchen this summer. It pairs particularly well with the Tuna Melt Tarts (see p.22).

## Serves 4

1lb 10oz (750g) new potatoes, roughly 15 small ones, scrubbed and cut in half
8oz (225g) vine-ripened tomatoes
cold-pressed canola oil
salt and freshly ground black pepper
2 tbsp Greek yogurt
2 tbsp garlic mayonnaise
juice of ½ lemon
handful of dill
handful of basil
3½oz (100g) Tuscan kale (or curly kale), tough stalks discarded, leaves finely chopped
1 shallot, finely chopped

1   Preheat the oven to 400°F (200°C).

2   Place the potatoes and tomatoes on a sheet pan, drizzle with canola oil, and season with salt and pepper. Roast for 30 minutes, until the potatoes are golden and tender. Remove from the oven and allow to cool.

3   To make the dressing, blitz the roasted tomatoes in a food processor with the yogurt, garlic mayonnaise, lemon juice, dill, basil, and some salt and pepper until fully combined.

4   Place the roasted potatoes, kale, and chopped shallots in a large bowl and drench with the tomato mayo dressing. Stir well until combined and serve.

**Soups, Salads, & Sides**

# Feta, Tomato, & Strawberry Panzanella Salad

This is the easiest salad to make but potentially one of my all-time favorites. It's like a cross between a Greek salad and a panzanella, and it's fabulously fresh and colorful. An added twist is the pickled red onion. Inspired by a recipe from my dear friend, and fellow Instagram foodie, Teri from *No Crumbs Left*, it is delightfully simple to make but does need a few hours to pickle. The salad would pair perfectly with the French Onion Soup Tarte Tatin (see p.56). Try to make it a good hour before serving and leave it at room temperature to enhance the flavors.

### Serves 4

4 slices of slightly stale crusty
  bread, torn into
  bite-size chunks
2 tbsp extra-virgin olive oil
4 tbsp garlic mayonnaise
4 large beef or vine tomatoes,
  roughly chopped
8–10 cherry tomatoes,
  cut in half
8–10 strawberries, cut
  into quarters
6½oz (190g) feta cheese,
  crumbled
handful of basil leaves
salt and freshly ground
  black pepper

### For the pickled onion:
1 red onion, finely sliced
  (preferably with
  a mandoline)
4 tbsp extra-virgin olive oil
2 tbsp cider vinegar
1 tsp balsamic vinegar
1 tsp honey
½ tsp black peppercorns
½ tsp Dijon mustard
½ tsp dried oregano

1 First make the pickled onion, which needs time to marinate. Place the onion in a bowl. Add the remaining ingredients to a separate bowl or jam jar and stir well. Pour the liquid over the onion and stir to ensure it is submerged. Cover and leave it to pickle for at least 12 hours before using. (The onion pickle will keep for at least 2 days in the fridge.)

2 When you're ready to make the salad, preheat the oven to 400°F (200°C).

3 Place the torn bread, olive oil, and garlic mayo in a large bowl and mix well so the bread is coated. Spread it out onto a sheet pan and cook in the oven for roughly 15 minutes, until just golden—you want the bread to be slightly soft still.

4 While the bread is in the oven, pop all the salad bits, except the feta and basil, into a large bowl. Spoon over 2 tablespoons of the pickled onion with some of the liquid (save the rest for another meal).

5 Once the bread is lightly golden, add it, while still hot, to the bowl containing the salad and stir well. Place the salad on a platter and sprinkle with the feta. Leave it to sit at room temperature for a good hour before serving to allow the flavors to mingle, if possible. Sprinkle with the basil leaves just before serving.

**Soups, Salads, & Sides**

# Fattoush-anella Salad

This magical salad is a delicious hybrid of the Mediterranean panzanella and the Middle Eastern fattoush, with an extra hit of crispy fried and pickled shallots. It is officially my salad of the summer! The multiple layers of the sumac-coated, oven-roasted pita bread with the fresh, herby salad and citrus-pickled shallot dressing make for an explosion of summery flavors. It would work wonderfully served with the Upside Down Spanakopita (see p.74).

## Serves 4

1 (8oz/225g) block of halloumi cheese, thickly sliced
1 romaine lettuce heart, chopped
4–5 vine tomatoes, chopped
4 mini cucumbers, chopped
5 radishes, thinly sliced
handful of cilantro, leaves chopped
handful of mint, leaves chopped

### For the quick pickle dressing:

6 shallots, cut in half lengthwise and thinly sliced
3 tbsp apple cider vinegar
4 tbsp extra-virgin olive oil
juice of ½ lemon
1 tsp fennel seeds
1 tsp dried oregano
1 tsp Dijon mustard

### For the crispy sumac pita:

3 whole wheat pita breads, torn into bite-size chunks
1 tsp sumac
1 tsp baharat
5 garlic cloves, peeled
pinch of sea salt
3 tbsp extra-virgin olive oil

### For the crispy shallots:

roughly 5 tbsp olive oil
6 shallots, thinly sliced
1 tbsp cornstarch

1   First make the quick pickle dressing. Place the shallots in a jar (they should fill it by two-thirds) and top with the rest of the ingredients. Place the lid on and shake vigorously until everything is combined. Chill in the fridge for 30 minutes. (They will keep for up to 2 weeks.)

2   To make the crispy sumac pita, preheat the oven to 400°F (200°C). Spread out the chunks of pita bread on a sheet pan lined with parchment paper. Sprinkle with the spices, garlic, and salt, then drizzle with the oil. Toss with your hands, ensuring the pita is coated in the spiced oil and bake for 25–35 minutes, turning once, or until wonderfully crisp. Set aside to cool.

3   To make the crispy shallots, place a heavy-bottomed sauté pan on medium heat and pour in a ½-in- (1-cm-) deep layer of oil. Meanwhile, toss the shallots in the cornstarch until coated. Carefully spoon the shallots into the hot oil and stir them with a wooden spoon. They will take roughly 8 minutes to crisp up, but keep an eye on them and give them the occasional stir, because they can go from golden to burned in seconds. Remove from the pan with a slotted spoon, drain well, and set aside on paper towels.

4   Time to build the salad. Cook the halloumi slices under the broiler for roughly 5 minutes on each side, until golden brown and slightly charred. Place all the ingredients for the salad in a serving bowl with the halloumi, then spoon the quick-pickled shallots on top, ensuring you spoon roughly 2 tablespoons of the pickling liquid over to make a dressing. Add the crispy pita and toss together until combined. Sprinkle with the crispy fried shallots and serve right away.

**Soups, Salads, & Sides**

# Brussels Sprout Caesar Salad

This twist on the classic is perfect for that sticky in-between Christmas and New Year week, when you still have a random bag of Brussels sprouts in the back of the fridge that needs using up but aren't sure what to do with it. I'm a huge Caesar salad fan and will order one if it's on the menu, but I am very picky about the dressing. For me, it's not necessarily about authenticity (as a lapsed vegetarian I am happy to do without the anchovy), but it has to be thick and tangy with a cheesy bite. I hate a limp, runny dressing—there's no call for it. I'd pair this salad with the Leftover Christmas Pie (see p.80).

## Serves 4

2 romaine lettuce hearts, sliced
10oz (300g) baby Brussels sprouts, sliced
⅔ cup (100g) frozen peas, defrosted
1 avocado, stone removed, peeled and chopped

### For the croutons/roasted sprouts:

5½oz (150g) slightly stale bread, torn into chunks
handful of Brussels sprouts, cut in half
drizzle of extra-virgin olive oil
drizzle of chili oil
salt and freshly ground black pepper
5½oz (150g) Parmesan cheese, finely grated, divided

### For the dressing:

2 tbsp Greek yogurt
1 tsp Dijon mustard
1 tsp olive oil
1 garlic clove
2 tbsp mayonnaise (see p.17), or use premade
juice and finely grated zest of ½ unwaxed lemon
1 tsp capers
large handful of chopped basil

1  First make the croutons/roasted sprouts. Preheat the oven to 400°F (200°C). Place the chunks of bread in a roasting pan along with the halved Brussels sprouts. Drizzle with a generous amount of olive oil and the chili oil, then season with salt and pepper. Sprinkle with 1¾oz (50g) of the Parmesan and toss well. Bake for roughly 20 minutes, turning occasionally, until the croutons are crisp and the sprouts slightly golden

2  To make the dressing, blitz all the ingredients in a blender with the remaining 3½oz (100g) of Parmesan until smooth. It needs to be on the tangy side of "blow your head off"! You may want to add some extra lemon juice or mayonnaise, depending on how creamy or tangy you like your dressing. Season generously with salt and pepper.

3  Now you can build your salad. I like to use the lettuce as a base, then throw in the raw sliced Brussels sprouts, peas, and avocado. Add a generous spoonful or two of the creamy dressing and then sprinkle with the crispy croutons and roasted sprouts at the end (still warm from the oven, if possible).

**Soups, Salads, & Sides**

# Right Side Up

Why upside down? Well, it really doesn't have to be, and in this chapter I extend the simple practice of layering delicious ingredients, but this time they're the right way up, so no flipping is needed. If you have an eternal fear of turning things over, then this collection of favorite one-pot meals is for you. Little can beat the textures and flavors of ingredients luxuriating in one pot, plus there's the added bonus of less washing up. Sure, there are a couple of extra sauces that need a little prep, but this is all about lazy days and enjoying time with your family and guests, rather than being stuck in front of the stove. One-pan cooking can span the seasons too—from richly succulent slow-cooked stews to quick and easy summery lasagnas. There's a one-pot meal to suit your mood and the time of the year.

# Chili Non-Carne Casserole

What I love most about this casserole is how simple it is to make, yet it delivers so much on taste. It's like the perfect baked potato, packed full of your favorite filling but all squeezed into one pan. There's something so comforting about a chili. It must have something to do with the heat of the chiles, plus the richness of the sauce that makes for such a fulfilling dish. Just a mention of its name feels wonderfully retro, and I love any dish that gives me a food memory hit.

## Serves 6

drizzle of extra-virgin olive oil
2 tbsp (30g) butter
1 red onion, roughly chopped
1 carrot, chopped
1 celery stalk, finely chopped
¼ fennel bulb, chopped (optional)
2 garlic cloves, finely grated
1 tsp ground cumin
1 tsp dried oregano
½ tsp dried chili flakes
1¼lb (500g) plant-based ground meat alternative
1 tsp smoked sweet paprika
½ tsp ajo chili powder or extra chili flakes
1 (14.5oz/400g) can diced tomatoes
1 tbsp tomato paste
¾ cup (175ml) red wine
2 cups (500ml) good-quality vegetable stock
1 (15.5oz/400g) can red kidney beans, drained
salt and freshly ground black pepper
5–6 medium potatoes, thickly sliced (unpeeled)
7oz (200g) sharp Cheddar cheese, grated
⅓ cup (100g) sour cream or Greek yogurt, to serve
1 handful of chopped cilantro, to finish

1  Heat the oil and butter in a large saucepan on medium heat and gently sauté the onion until softened. Add the carrot, celery, and fennel (if using) and sauté for another 5 minutes, then stir in the garlic, cumin, oregano, and chili flakes.

2  With the heat still on medium, add the plant-based ground meat alternative and cook quickly, stirring regularly, until browned, then add the paprika and chili powder.

3  Add the diced tomatoes, tomato paste, and red wine, followed by the vegetable stock. Stir, turn the heat down slightly and let it gently bubble away for 15 minutes before adding the kidney beans. Add a pinch of salt, turn the heat down to its lowest setting, and simmer for at least 50 minutes, until rich and thickened.

4  Meanwhile, par-boil the potatoes in a large pan of boiling water for 3 minutes—you don't want them too soft but tender enough that they yield easily when prodded with a fork. Drain well and set aside to cool slightly.

5  Preheat the oven to 400°F (200°C).

6  Assemble in a large, shallow casserole dish or roasting pan, starting with a layer of the chili, followed by a layer of potatoes, then drizzle with a little oil. Season with salt and pepper, then add a layer of grated cheese. Repeat until you've used up all the ingredients or your pan is full. You want to end with a layer of potato on top and save a handful of grated cheese for later. (You may have a little of the chili left over, which is perfect for freezing and will keep for up to 3 months.)

7  Drizzle more olive oil over the top layer of potatoes, cover the pan with a lid or foil, and bake for 30 minutes, then remove the lid/foil, add a final sprinkling of grated cheese, and bake for a further 20 minutes, or until golden and bubbling on top. Serve with a good spoonful of the sour cream or yogurt and finish with a sprinkling of cilantro.

**Right Side Up**

**126**

# Chicken Thigh Risotto

There's absolutely no way I could write a cookbook without including my beloved chicken thighs. For me, they are the best part of a chicken, hands down, no argument, but I insist you buy them with the bone in and skin on. There's a layer of wonderful fat under the skin that adds so much flavor to this one-pot dish.

**Serves 4**

1 large white onion, cut into
    8 wedges
2 celery stalks, chopped
1 large carrot, cut lengthwise
    in half, then cut into chunks
8 garlic cloves, skin on (life is
    too short to peel)
salt and freshly ground
    black pepper
2 sprigs of rosemary, leaves
    picked
2 sprigs of thyme, leaves
    picked
drizzle of extra-virgin olive oil
8 bone-in, skin-on free-range
    chicken thighs
⅓ cup (100ml) white wine
    or chicken stock
5½oz (150g) arborio
    (risotto) rice

**1**   Preheat the oven to 350°F (180°C).

**2**   Place the onion, celery, carrot, and garlic in a large, shallow casserole dish or Dutch oven, season well with salt and pepper, and sprinkle on the herbs. Drizzle with a little olive oil (you really don't need much fat because a lot comes from the thighs) and then mix everything together with your hands.

**3**   Sit the chicken thighs on top of the vegetables, skin side down. You may have to wedge them in like a jigsaw, but they will fit and the dish will reduce down as it cooks. Wash your hands well, then pour over the white wine or stock, and season again with a generous amount of salt and pepper. Cover with the lid or foil and bake for 45 minutes.

**4**   Take the casserole dish out of the oven, take the lid/foil off, and carefully remove the chicken thighs. Add in the rice and stir well. Place the chicken thighs back on top, skin side up. Season generously with salt and pepper, return the lid/foil, and put the casserole dish back in the oven for a further 20 minutes.

**5**   Turn the oven up to 400°F (200°C). Remove the lid/foil from the casserole dish, add a splash of water if the rice looks too dry, then cook for a further 15 minutes, until the chicken skin is gloriously crisp. It should be a good golden color and the rice will have absorbed the cooking liquid. If the skin is not crispy enough, just put the casserole dish back in the oven for another few minutes—believe me, these thighs can take it!

**6**   And that's it ... I like to place the casserole dish in the middle of the table with a big spoon and let everyone help themselves. Serve it as is or maybe steam something green to go with it.

**Right Side Up**

# Sun-Dried Tomato Pesto, Sausage, & Cauliflower Bake

I think we all have those moments when the fridge seems full of half-used vegetables that either need throwing out or using up quickly. An all-in-one meal, like this stunning one, is a useful and tasty way to use everything up at once. It's quick, easy, and very tasty, and works with pretty much any vegetables you have lurking around.

**Serves 4**

½ large cauliflower, cut into florets (leaves on)
1 large carrot, cut into wedges
1 bunch asparagus or 1 zucchini (depending on the season)
handful of brown button mushrooms, cut in half
2 shallots, cut into quarters
8 sausages (veggie or meat)
1 (15.5oz/400g) can lima beans, drained
2 tbsp Greek yogurt
salt and freshly ground black pepper

**For the sun-dried tomato pesto:**

1oz (30g) fresh basil, plus extra to finish
2 garlic cloves
⅓ cup (50g) pine nuts, toasted
1¾oz (50g) sharp Cheddar cheese, finely grated
9oz (250g) sun-dried tomatoes in oil, drained
3 tbsp extra-virgin olive oil

1   First make the pesto. Place all the ingredients in a food processor and blend to a rough paste (you may need to add a little more oil). Taste to check if the balance of flavors is to your liking. Add more cheese or basil, if needed, and blend again. Set aside.

2   Preheat the oven to 375°F (190°C).

3   Place all the vegetables in a large bowl, pour over half of the pesto and mix well, add the sausages and mix again. Spread out the mixture on a large sheet pan or roasting pan and bake for 25 minutes.

4   Remove from the oven and spoon in the lima beans along with half of the remaining pesto. Stir everything to combine and place it back in the oven for another 25 minutes, or until darkly golden.

5   In a bowl, mix the Greek yogurt into the remaining pesto. Serve the vegetables and sausages with a spoonful of the pesto by the side and finish with a sprinkling of basil leaves.

**Right Side Up**

# Creamy Mushroom Oven-Baked Orzotto

In the summer of 2022, the baked feta pasta sauce became a viral sensation on social media, and I can see why. A block of feta roasted with a handful of cherry tomatoes, garlic, olive oil, and herbs and you have a wonderfully quick and simple pasta sauce. The challenge for me is that many find feta too salty, so I wanted to create a simple and tasty alternative using garlic and herb cream cheese, but you could use any creamy soft cheese you love.

**Serves 2**

1 onion, finely chopped
5½oz (150g) mushrooms (a mix of baby portobello and brown button mushrooms)
2 garlic cloves, skin on
2 tsp fresh thyme leaves or 1 tsp dried
salt and freshly ground black pepper
drizzle of extra-virgin olive oil
5½oz (150g) garlic and herb cream cheese
7oz (200g) dried orzo pasta
1 cup (200ml) boiling water (you may need a little more)
⅔ cup (100g) frozen peas

**1** Preheat the oven to 400°F (200°C).

**2** Place the onion, mushrooms, garlic, and thyme in an ovenproof dish and season well with salt and pepper. Drizzle with olive oil and stir well. Bake for 20 minutes, then spoon over dollops of the cream cheese and return the dish to the oven for another 10 minutes.

**3** Sprinkle the orzo into the dish and stir everything together. As you stir, squeeze the soft roasted garlic out of its skin (discard the skins). Carefully pour in the boiling water and stir to mix everything together. Return to the oven for a further 10–15 minutes, depending on how *al dente* you like your pasta.

**4** Halfway through the baking time, stir in the frozen peas (you may at this stage need to add a little more water—just ½ cup (120ml) should do it—then return the dish to the oven for another 5 minutes, or until the peas are tender and heated through.

**Right Side Up**

# Zucchini, Asparagus, & Eggplant Parmigiana

This twist on the classic *melanzane*, or eggplant parmigiana, was taught to me by an Italian photographer while on a shoot around 20 years ago, which sounds as wonderfully glamorous as it was! Listening to him describe the way his Nonna used to make it is one of the best food memories I have. It has become one of my favorite go-to summer meals but, I warn you now, it's not a quick dish to make because you need to make my special slow-cooked tomato sauce first. Wait for a rainy summer day to spend some time in the kitchen and create this stunner.

**Serves 6**

1 tsp dried oregano
1 tsp smoked sweet paprika (optional)
1 cup (120g) all-purpose flour
1 large egg, beaten with a little milk
3 large zucchini, thickly sliced lengthwise
½ eggplant, cut into disks
8 asparagus spears, trimmed
vegetable oil, for frying
1 recipe quantity of Slow-Cooked Tomato Sauce (see p.16), or use premade
4½oz (125g) mozzarella cheese, drained and torn into pieces
7oz (200g) Parmesan cheese, finely grated
salt and freshly ground black pepper

1 Mix the oregano and paprika (if using) into the flour on a plate. Pour the beaten egg mixture into a rectangular dish. Dip the zucchini, eggplant, and asparagus first into the egg mixture and then the flour mixture until lightly coated. Tap off any excess flour.

2 In a large, deep skillet, heat enough vegetable oil over medium heat to shallow fry the vegetables. Fry 3 pieces at a time—don't be tempted to overcrowd the pan, or the vegetables won't turn golden and crisp. Set aside on paper towels to drain off any excess oil while you fry all the vegetables.

3 Preheat the oven to 375°F (190°C).

4 You're now ready to assemble the dish. Start with a layer of zucchini, then add some of the slow-cooked tomato sauce, followed by one-third of the mozzarella, and a large handful of grated Parmesan, arranging them in a medium-size ovenproof casserole dish. Season well with salt and pepper.

5 Repeat with a layer each of eggplant and asparagus, interspersing them with the tomato sauce and finishing with the final third of mozzarella and Parmesan. Season well with salt and pepper between each vegetable layer. Bake for 30 minutes, until you have a golden, bubbling dish.

**Right Side Up**

# Veggie Sausage, Shallot, & Bean Tagliatelle Bake

My love for the humble shallot knows no bounds. It's fair to say that I prefer this little onion to its other family members, and that even includes garlic. The wonderful sweet, light onion flavor it lends to all kinds of dishes is second to none, then add in a slight caramelization and you have golden nuggets of flavor that add a touch of sophistication to any dish. This sausage pasta bake is such a simple recipe. Everything gets roasted together until perfectly bronzed and then you throw in some tagliatelle, spinach, and a little cream for extra indulgence.

**Serves 2–3**

6 vegetarian sausages, thickly sliced
8 shallots, cut into quarters lengthwise
10oz (300g) canned lima beans, drained
8 olives with pimento, chopped
1 sprig of rosemary, leaves picked
salt and freshly ground black pepper
drizzle of extra-virgin olive oil
10oz (300g) fresh tagliatelle
3½oz (100g) fresh spinach
1 cup (250ml) heavy cream
Parmesan cheese, finely grated, to serve

1  Preheat the oven to 400°F (200°C).

2  Place the sausages, shallots, lima beans, and olives in a roasting pan. Sprinkle in the rosemary and season well with salt and pepper. Drizzle olive oil in and mix well, ensuring everything is coated, then spread out evenly in the pan. Bake for 30–40 minutes, turning once, until bronzed and beautiful. Remove from the oven and stir.

3  Meanwhile, cook the pasta following the instructions on the package. Fresh pasta takes just a minute or two to cook in boiling water. Place a steamer basket over the top of the pasta pan to steam the spinach for a minute at the same time.

4  Pour the cream into the roasting pan, followed by the drained pasta and spinach. Mix well and pop the pan back into the oven for another 5 minutes before serving with some freshly grated Parmesan on top.

**Right Side Up**

# Summer Veggie Lasagna

Living in the UK, the season of "summer" can mean many things, much of it to do with rain. It can literally be blazing sunshine in the morning and then cold and rainy in the evening, which can be frustrating for many reasons, but in particular it makes it hard to plan outdoor summer events. It may have been barbecue weather yesterday, but it's most definitely comfort food today, and that's where this luscious lasagna comes in. It has the richness and warming qualities of the regular version but uses layers of summer vegetables in a light, creamy cheese sauce.

## Serves 4–6

2 tbsp (30g) butter
drizzle of extra-virgin olive oil
4 shallots, cut into quarters lengthwise
1 zucchini, thickly sliced
2 sprigs of rosemary, leaves picked
2 sprigs of thyme, leaves picked
salt and freshly ground black pepper
8 asparagus spears, trimmed, stalks chopped and tips left whole
handful of green beans, trimmed and sliced
⅔ cup (100g) frozen peas
3½oz (100g) sharp Cheddar cheese, grated
3½oz (100g) red Leicester cheese, grated
6–8 lasagna sheets (I use fresh pasta)

### For the cheese sauce:
2 cups (500ml) whole milk
⅓ cup (50g) all-purpose flour
3 tbsp (50g) butter
5½oz (150g) garlic and herb cream cheese

**1** In a large saucepan, melt the butter with the olive oil on medium heat, then throw in the shallots and zucchini and sauté for 6 minutes, or until softened and starting to color.

**2** Stir in the herbs and season with salt and pepper, then add the asparagus and green beans and stir well. Lastly, add in the frozen peas, pop the lid on, and turn off the heat. Leave the pan to sit on the stove while you make the cheese sauce.

**3** Place the milk, flour, and butter in a separate pan on medium-low heat and, using a balloon whisk, stir continuously for about 5 minutes, until the sauce begins to thicken. Turn the heat down to the lowest setting and let the sauce gently bubble away for another 3 minutes, whisking occasionally. Once beautifully thick, take the pan off the heat and allow it to stand for 1 minute, then stir in the cream cheese.

**4** Preheat the oven to 400°F (200°C).

**5** To assemble the lasagna, arrange a layer of the cheese sauce, vegetables, grated cheeses, and pasta sheets in a large, deep ovenproof dish and repeat until you have 3 layers, finishing with a layer of the cheese sauce and a sprinkling of cheese. Bake for 20–25 minutes, until the top is wonderfully bubbling and golden.

**Right Side Up**

# Spinach, Pea, & Sausage Eggs Florentine

I adore shakshuka; soft poached eggs nestled in a rich and spicy tomato sauce—what's not to like? A lot, apparently, because my husband, The Viking, refuses to eat eggs with tomatoes. He can't even be in the same room when they're served together, let alone have them on the same plate! So the search continues for the perfect brunch dish. This recipe uses green veggies instead of tomatoes and takes the fuss away by cooking everything in one pan, yet it still gives you wonderfully soft coddled eggs.

## Serves 4

6 chipolata sausages, cut into
   small bite-size chunks
drizzle of extra-virgin olive oil
1 onion, finely chopped
2 tbsp (30g) butter
2 sprigs of lemon thyme or
   regular thyme, leaves picked
1lb 2oz (500g) frozen spinach
3⅓ cups (500g) frozen peas
handful of green pitted olives,
   cut in half
⅔ cup (150ml) heavy cream
⅓ cup (100ml) whole milk
salt and freshly ground
   black pepper
4 eggs
thick slices of toasted
   sourdough, to serve
   (optional)

1 In a large, wide, shallow saucepan (with a lid) or casserole dish, sauté the sausages in a little olive oil over medium heat. As the sausages begin to brown, add the onion, butter, and thyme and sauté until softened.

2 Turn the heat to low, add the spinach and cook, covered, for 5 minutes. Take the lid off, stir in the peas and olives and continue to cook for another 5–10 minutes, until any water from the spinach has evaporated. Add the cream and milk, and cook for a further 5 minutes, stirring at intervals, then season well.

3 Make four wells in the spinach mixture. Crack in the eggs, cover with the lid and continue to cook for 5 minutes, or until the whites have set but the yolks remain runny. Serve with thick slices of sourdough bread, pan-fried in butter, if you like—pure brunch heaven.

**Right Side Up**

# Tumbet Savory Crumble

We're fortunate enough to spend a lot of time on the beautiful Balearic Island of Mallorca, where we regularly feast on the stunning local cuisine. *Tumbet* (pronounced toombet) is a traditional vegetable dish, consisting of layers of sliced potato, eggplant, and red pepper that have been fried in olive oil and served in a rich tomato sauce. It's often served with pan-fried local fish or roast goat or lamb, which are very popular, but it also makes a wonderful vegetarian main dish. I've created a savory crumble topping using a local rye bread to soak up all the wonderful sauce. You can cook it in the traditional terra-cotta dish, called a *cazuela*, if you have one.

## Serves 6

1 eggplant, thickly sliced
1 zucchini, thickly sliced
1 large red bell pepper, seeded and chopped into large chunks
4 potatoes, thickly sliced
drizzle of extra-virgin olive oil
2 garlic cloves, finely chopped
2 sprigs of rosemary, leaves picked
salt and freshly ground black pepper
1 recipe quantity of Slow-Cooked Tomato Sauce (see p.16), or use premade

### For the crumble topping:
3½oz (100g) slightly stale bread, such as sourdough or rye, which is more traditional
3½oz (100g) Mahón cheese (Parmesan also works well), finely grated
6 tbsp (100g) cold butter, cut into small pieces

**1** Preheat the oven to 375°F (190°C).

**2** To make the crumble, place the ingredients in a food processor and blitz to a coarse crumb texture. Set aside.

**3** Add all the vegetables to 1 or 2 large roasting pans, drizzle over some olive oil and sprinkle in the garlic and rosemary. Season with salt and pepper. Bake for about 1 hour, turning the vegetables halfway, or until softened and starting to color but not too much. Turn the oven off and let the vegetables cool completely in the oven.

**4** To assemble the dish, place a ladleful of the tomato sauce in the bottom of a large ovenproof dish, then add a layer of the roasted vegetables, followed by another layer of sauce and then vegetables. Keep going until the sauce and vegetables have all been used up. Traditionally, you would layer each vegetable separately, but feel free to be creative.

**5** Sprinkle on the crumble mixture and bake for 45 minutes, until gloriously golden and bubbling. I like to serve it lukewarm, rather than straight from the oven, because you can taste the individual flavors better.

**Right Side Up**

# Last of the Summer Veggie Stew & Dumplings

This one-pot wonder is a celebration of the transition from summer to fall. It uses up the last of the sweet fresh summer vegetables, such as new potatoes, green beans, and zucchini, which are simmered in a light white-wine-based broth. It's also hearty enough for those cooler evenings with fluffy, cheesy, herb dumplings sitting on top. It's one of my go-to dishes that I make time and time again, depending on which veggies are in season and what I want to eat. As the season turns to winter, I'll add more root vegetables, such as rutabaga and parsnips or cabbage and cauliflower, but for now I'm keeping it light and fresh.

## Serves 4

1 tbsp extra-virgin olive oil
1 red onion, chopped
about 6 button mushrooms, cut in half
1 zucchini, chopped
1 tsp chopped rosemary
2 garlic cloves, finely grated
salt and freshly ground black pepper
1 carrot, cut into batons
6 new potatoes, chopped
½ cup (100g) green beans, cut in half
1 tbsp all-purpose flour
3¼ cups (800ml) good-quality vegetable stock
1 cup (200ml) white wine
¼ cup (50g) frozen peas

### For the cheesy herb dumplings:

1½ cups (200g) all-purpose flour
1½ tsp baking powder
1 tsp salt
6 tbsp (100g) cold butter, cut into small cubes
1¾oz (50g) sharp Cheddar cheese, coarsely grated
1 tsp Herbs de Provence

1 Place a large, ovenproof, shallow saucepan (with a lid) or casserole on medium-low heat, pour in the olive oil, and sauté the onion for roughly 5 minutes, until softened. Stir in the mushrooms and zucchini and sauté for another 5 minutes, until they get a little bit of color. Add the rosemary and garlic and stir well. Season with a generous pinch of salt and pepper.

2 Add the carrot, new potatoes, and green beans to the pan and stir well. Cover with the lid, turn the heat down to its lowest setting and let the vegetables sweat for 5 minutes.

3 Remove the lid, stir in the all-purpose flour, then pour in the stock and white wine. Increase the heat slightly and bring the liquid to a boil, then reduce the heat to its lowest setting and let it gently simmer for at least 30 minutes with the lid on. Stir in the peas at the end.

4 While the stew is simmering away, make the dumplings. Place all the ingredients in a large bowl and season well with salt and pepper. Add a little cold water and bring the mixture together with your fingertips to form a soft dough. Keep it all light and quick and try not to overwork the dough. Divide the dough roughly into 8–10 small balls and sit them on the top of the stew so they are half submerged. Cover with the lid and cook on low heat for 15 minutes, until the dumplings are light and fluffy.

5 For a golden finish on top, heat the broiler to high. Take the lid off and place the pan under the broiler for another 5 minutes, until the dumplings start to crisp.

**Note:** This is the kind of dish that always tastes better made ahead. Make the stew the day before serving, leave it to cool, and place somewhere where nobody can take a spoonful. Prepare the dumplings fresh on the day and reheat the stew before putting the dumplings on top to cook.

**144**

# Roast in the Hole

My husband believes that anything served between two slices of bread is the best thing in the world. I can go one step further and say anything immersed in a Yorkshire pudding batter is better! To prove a point, I've created this recipe, which is the very happy love-child of a Sunday roast and the comfort-food classic, toad in the hole. It's a simple egg batter, but once it mingles with all those incredible meat juices it becomes the most joyful savory pudding and fit for any dinner table.

## Serves 4

1 large carrot, roughly chopped
8 brown button mushrooms,
    cut into quarters
2 large celery stalks,
    roughly chopped
1 onion, roughly chopped
3–4 Yukon Gold or other white
    potatoes, peeled and cut into
    large chunks
3 sprigs of rosemary,
    leaves picked
3 sprigs of thyme,
    leaves picked
salt and freshly ground
    black pepper
drizzle of extra-virgin olive oil
4 skin-on, bone-in chicken
    portions, such as legs
    or thighs
4 sausages, cut in half
    crosswise

### For the Yorkshire pudding mix:

4 eggs
1 cup (140g) all-purpose flour
1 cup (200ml) whole milk

**1**   Preheat the oven to 425°F (220°C).

**2**   Put the vegetables into a large, deep roasting pan. Spread them out evenly, then sprinkle in the herbs and season well with salt and pepper. Drizzle with a little oil, then place the chicken portions, skin side down, and sausages on top. Drizzle with a little more oil and season the top of the chicken pieces with salt and pepper.

**3**   Cover the pan with foil and roast 30 minutes, or until the vegetables have softened, then remove the foil, turn the chicken over and roast for a further 15 minutes, until the chicken skin is golden. There should be plenty of gorgeous chicken juices in the bottom of the roasting pan.

**4**   Meanwhile, make the Yorkshire pudding batter. In a large bowl, beat the eggs into the flour using a balloon whisk, then add the milk. Season with salt and pepper and whisk again until you have a smooth batter. Set aside to rest.

**5**   When the chicken is ready, pour the batter over the roasted veggies and between the chicken pieces. Place the pan back in the oven for another 30 minutes, or until the batter has risen and turned golden brown.

**Right Side Up**

# Roasted Potato, Beef, & Bean Hot Pot

If you're looking for an easy but insanely delicious one-pot meal to serve for a cozy Sunday lunch with the family, then look no further than my twist on the classic Lancashire hot pot, which is traditionally made with lamb and has a layer of golden sliced potato on top. My version gives me an excuse to make my fave potatoes without the trouble of roasting them in a separate dish.

**Serves 4**

8 Yukon Gold potatoes, peeled and cut into bite-size chunks
4 tbsp extra-virgin olive oil, divided
1 tsp Herbs de Provence
salt and freshly ground black pepper
2 tbsp (30g) butter
14oz (400g) diced braising steak
1 red onion, roughly chopped
2 carrots, roughly chopped
2 celery stalks, chopped
½ fennel bulb, roughly chopped
2 garlic cloves, finely chopped
2 sprigs of rosemary, leaves chopped
2 sprigs of thyme, leaves chopped
2 tsp all-purpose flour
2 cups (500ml) vegetable stock
2 cups (500ml) dry white wine
1 (15.5oz/400g) can lima beans, drained
½ Napa cabbage, roughly chopped
1 tsp brewer's yeast (or Marmite)
1 tbsp ketchup

1  Par-boil the potatoes in boiling water for 6 minutes, until just beginning to soften. Drain well, then put the potatoes back into the pan and add 2 tbsp of the olive oil and the Herbs de Provence. Season with salt and pepper. Cover with the lid and jiggle the pan vigorously a few times until the potatoes get lovely fluffy edges, which will make them nice and crispy when roasted. Leave the lid on and set aside while you make the stew.

2  Place a large, shallow cast-iron pan or ovenproof sauté pan (with a lid) on medium heat, add the remaining olive oil and the butter and, once hot, add the beef and cook until browned and caramelized all over. Remove the beef from the pan with a slotted spoon and set aside.

3  Add a little more oil to the pan, followed by the onion, carrots, celery, and fennel and sauté for roughly 6 minutes, until softened slightly.

4  Stir in the garlic and fresh herbs. Cover with the lid and let the vegetables sweat for 10 minutes, until softened.

5  Return the beef to the pan and stir in the flour. Pour in the stock and wine and let it bubble away for roughly 5 minutes, until thickened slightly. Stir in the lima beans, cabbage, yeast extract, and ketchup. Cover with the lid, turn the heat down to low, and let the stew gently simmer for 30 minutes.

6  Meanwhile, preheat the oven to 400°F (200°C).

7  Arrange the par-boiled potatoes on top of the stew, then place the pan in the oven, with the lid off. Cook for another 40–50 minutes, until the potatoes are crisp and golden, and the beef stew is thick and unctuous.

**Right Side Up**

# Marmalade & Blood Orange Chicken Bake

There's some kind of alchemy that happens when you cook chicken with oranges, especially if using the fattier parts of the bird, such as the thighs. I think it's the citrus twang that cuts through the rich meat so beautifully that I love. The great thing about marmalade is that it's already prepared for you, so all you do is slather it over whatever you're cooking. Job done!

## Serves 4

8 bone-in, skin-on, free-range chicken thighs
4–5 tbsp of your favorite marmalade (I use a three-fruit marmalade, which is divine)
1 carrot, roughly chopped
1 large onion, cut into wedges
1 uncooked beet, cut into wedges
5 garlic cloves, skin on
1 (15.5oz/400g) can lima beans, drained
2 sprigs of rosemary, leaves picked
2 sprigs of lemon thyme, leaves picked
salt and freshly ground black pepper
1 cup (250ml) white wine
2 cups (500ml) good-quality chicken stock, divided
drizzle of extra-virgin olive oil
1 blood orange (or use a regular orange if not in season), cut into wedges

1   Preheat the oven to 400°F (200°C).

2   Place the chicken thighs in a bowl with the marmalade and rub it all together with your hands until the thighs are fully coated.

3   Place all the chopped vegetables and garlic in a roasting pan and spread out evenly. Sprinkle in the lima beans and herbs, then season well with salt and pepper.

4   Place the marmalade-coated chicken thighs on top, skin side up, pour in the wine and half the stock. Drizzle with a little oil. Season well again with salt and pepper and slot the orange wedges between the thighs. Cover tightly with foil and pop into the oven for 1 hour.

5   Remove the foil, carefully pick out the garlic cloves and squeeze the flesh out of the skin into the pan. Stir, adding a splash more of the stock if it's looking a little dry, then return to the oven for a further 30 minutes, until the thighs are gloriously golden and cooked through.

**Right Side Up**

**150**

# Sausage Cobbler

We found our cottage in Lincolnshire more than 20 years ago and it became our little secret haven where we could escape the craziness of London into the wilds. When we first moved here, the county was quite bad at celebrating all it has to offer, including its incredible local produce, but over the years it has shrugged off the shyness and started shouting far and wide. Packed with herbs and the best-quality, locally reared pork, Lincolnshire sausages make a brilliant addition to this comforting savory-scone-topped stew.

## Serves 4–6

3 shallots, peeled and cut in half lengthwise
1 celery stalk, chopped
1 carrot, cut into batons
1 beet, cut into quarters
½ cup (50g) green beans, chopped
1 Russet potato, peeled and cut into bite-size chunks
5 garlic cloves, skin removed
2 sprigs of rosemary, leaves chopped
2 sprigs of thyme, leaves chopped
2 tbsp extra-virgin olive oil
salt and freshly ground black pepper
6 garlic or herb sausages
1 tbsp all-purpose flour
⅓ cup (100ml) white wine
2 cups (500ml) vegetable stock
1 tsp tomato paste

### For the cobbler topping:
1¾ cups (225g) all-purpose flour
2 tsp baking powder
1 tsp salt
3 tbsp (50g) cold butter, cut into small cubes
1¾oz (50g) sharp Cheddar cheese, finely grated
1 tbsp mix of finely chopped rosemary and thyme
splash of whole milk

**1** Preheat the oven to 400°F (200°C).

**2** Place all the vegetables in a large, shallow casserole or ovenproof dish with the garlic and herbs. Add the olive oil and season with salt and pepper. Lay the sausages on top and pop it into the oven for 30 minutes, uncovered.

**3** While the vegetables are cooking, make the cobbler dough. Place the flour, baking powder, salt, butter, and cheese in a bowl and rub together until it resembles fine breadcrumbs. Mix in the herbs, then season with salt and pepper. Stir in a splash of milk with a fork until the mixture starts to come together into a ball. You want the dough to be fairly soft, so add a little more milk if you think it looks too firm. Set aside.

**4** Take the casserole out of the oven, sprinkle in the all-purpose flour and stir well. Add the wine, stock, and tomato paste and stir until combined.

**5** I like my cobbler nicely rustic so I pull off handfuls of the dough and form them into rough balls, or you can press the dough out on a floured work surface until it is about 2 in (5 cm) thick and use a scone cutter to stamp out rounds. Sit the dumplings on top of the stew, and pop it back in the oven, uncovered, for 20 minutes, until risen and golden. Serve in deep bowls.

**Right Side Up**

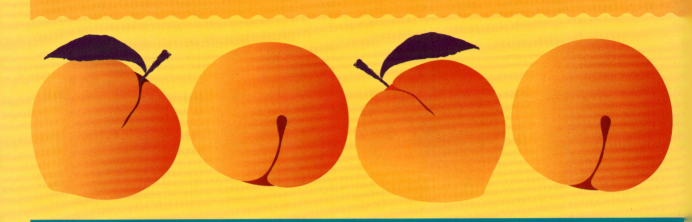

# Cakes & Desserts

I hate to have to admit it, but I didn't invent the art of cooking upside down. I know, a shock, right! The classic apple tarte tatin has been a staple of French cuisine for well over a hundred years. However, whoever came up with the idea of replacing the layer of pastry with a cake batter was a genius and deserves all the medals. There's something so wonderfully indulgent about digging into the hidden layer of fruit languishing under a light vanilla cake. It's like opening Christmas presents and birthday presents all on the same day! Yet, this chapter isn't just about upside-down cakes (although there's no need to worry, I've included a version of the classic pineapple one); it also features puddings, bars, and desserts that need flipping right-side up before serving. Who knew there were so many of them? From the bundt cake to a gelatin mold, it's time to turn over a new upside-down leaf.

# Apricot, Polenta, & Almond Cake

There's a wonderful brief moment in the summer fruit season when special apricots are in the shops. You know they are special because they're flushed with the most divine blush of color, it's as though they're slightly embarrassed at how divine they taste. That's the moment to make this sheet cake. Like those apricots, it looks divine and is just a little bit erotic. It's also embarrassingly simple to make.

## Serves 8

1 cup plus 3 tbsp (225g) sugar,
   plus extra for sprinkling
1 cup (225g) salted butter,
   softened
1¼ cups (125g) ground
   almonds
¾ cup plus 2 tbsp (100g) fine
   polenta
1 tsp baking powder
3 large eggs
finely grated zest of
   1 unwaxed lemon
10 apricots, cut in half
   lengthwise, stones removed

### YOU WILL NEED
13 x 9 in (32 x 23 cm) sheet
   pan, base and sides
   greased and lined with
   parchment paper

1. Preheat the oven to 400°F (200°C). Sprinkle the bottom of the lined tray with a little sugar and set aside.

2. In a large bowl, beat the butter and sugar with an electric hand mixer or in a stand mixer for about 5 minutes, until pale and fluffy.

3. In a separate bowl, mix together the ground almonds, polenta, and baking powder, and beat a quarter into the butter-sugar mixture. Whisk in one of the eggs, then alternate between the dry ingredients and eggs, beating continuously to a smooth cake batter. Finally, fold in the lemon zest.

4. Lay the apricots, cut side down, in the bottom of the prepared pan and carefully spoon the cake mixture on top of the fruit to cover. Spread it out gently, taking care not to move the apricots.

5. Bake for 35–40 minutes, until risen and golden, and a skewer comes out clean when inserted into the middle. The edges of the cake will also start to shrink away from the sides of the pan.

6. Leave the cake to cool completely in the pan on a wire rack. Lay a large cutting board or platter on top and flip it over. Carefully peel off the backing paper and cut the cake into squares to serve.

# Pineapple & Rum Cake

I could hardly write a book about upside-down cooking without including a recipe for this wonderfully retro pineapple upside down cake. It's a classic for a reason but, of course, I've given it a twist by adding a splash or two of my favorite dark spiced rum.

**Serves 8**

1 cup (225) salted butter, softened, plus extra for greasing
2 tbsp dark brown sugar
6–8 canned pineapple rings
9–11 black cherries in kirsch
1¼ cup (150g) all-purpose flour, sifted
1 tsp baking powder
½ tsp salt
1 cup plus 3 tbsp (225g) sugar
¾ cup (75g) ground almonds
1 tsp vanilla paste
3 large eggs
3 tbsp dark spiced rum

**YOU WILL NEED**
13 x 9 in (32 x 23 cm) sheet pan, base and sides greased and lined with parchment paper

**1** Preheat the oven to 400°F (200°C).

**2** Rub a generous amount of butter over the lined pan and sprinkle with the brown sugar. Arrange the pineapple slices in the base of the pan (you may need to cut some in half to fit them in a single layer). Fill each pineapple ring with a cherry, and then dot one in each of the spaces between.

**3** In a large bowl, beat the flour, baking powder, salt, butter, sugar, ground almonds, vanilla, and eggs together with an electric hand mixer or in a stand mixer to a smooth cake batter. Pour in the rum to thin it a little and beat again until combined.

**4** Carefully spoon the cake mixture over the cherry-studded pineapple rings—it will only just cover the fruit, so spread it out gently.

**5** Bake for 30 minutes, until risen and golden, and a skewer comes out cleanish when inserted into the middle. Leave to cool completely in the pan on a wire rack. Ease a spatula around the edge of the pan, place a cutting board on top and, with one deft move, flip it. Carefully peel off the backing paper before cutting the cake into squares.

**Cakes & Desserts**

# Banana, Coffee, & Cinnamon Cake

We've just got back from California and one of the things that really sticks in my mind is the overwhelming aroma of banana, cinnamon, and coffee that seems to waft like a comforting fog in the air as you walk around the wonderful cafes, bars, and bakeries. There's a sweetness to it that is captivating yet not cloying. It lures you in so you're desperate to purchase. It's capitalism in cake form. I wanted to capture this in my own cake, so I've combined everything using the all-in-one method. It's like banana bread on steroids and it is glorious.

## Serves 8

3 large eggs, beaten
2 ripe bananas, mashed with a fork
1½ cups (200g) all-purpose flour, sifted
2 tsp baking powder
¾ tsp salt
14 tbsp (200g) salted butter, softened
1 cup (200g) sugar
1 tbsp ground cinnamon
double shot of freshly made espresso, about 4 tbsp, left to cool
1 tsp vanilla extract

### For the espresso glaze:
single shot of freshly made espresso, about 2 tbsp, left to cool
powdered sugar, sifted

### YOU WILL NEED
10-cup (4 pint/2.3 liter) tube pan; or 8-in (20-cm) round cake pan, greased and lined with parchment paper

1   Preheat the oven to 350°F (180°C).

2   In a large bowl, beat all the ingredients, except those for the glaze, until well combined and fluffy. This will take about 3 minutes on medium speed in a stand mixer with the paddle attachment, or you can use an electric hand mixer. Put the cake batter into your pan and level the top.

3   Bake for 45–55 minutes, until risen, golden, and springy to the touch. Leave the cake to cool completely in the pan, then turn it out onto a wire rack or a plate.

4   To make the espresso glaze, mix the cooled espresso with enough powdered sugar to form a thick glaze. Drizzle the icing over the cake before serving.

# Blueberry & Apple Muffin Cake

This is one of my most requested cakes. It's more like a muffin because it's a little denser than a regular cake and could be served for breakfast—but if I'm honest I could eat any cake for breakfast! The bottom eventually becomes the top, so we start with a base of crumble and then layer the fruit and cake on top.

## Serves 8

1 cup (225g) butter, softened
1 cup (125g) all-purpose flour
½ tsp salt
scant ½ cup (50g) whole wheat flour
2 tsp baking powder
½ cup (50g) ground almonds
1 cup plus 3 tbsp (225g) sugar
3 large eggs, lightly beaten
1 tsp vanilla paste
2 apples, peeled, cored and chopped into small pieces
3½oz (100g) blueberries

### For the crumble topping:
10 tbsp (150g) cold salted butter, cut into small cubes
½ cup (100g) sugar
¼ cup (50g) demerara sugar
1 cup (100g) old-fashioned rolled oats
1¼ cup (150g) all-purpose flour
½ cup (50g) ground almonds
3½oz (100g) blueberries

### For the icing:
juice of 1 lemon
1¾ cups (200g) powdered sugar, sifted

### YOU WILL NEED
12 x 8 in (30 x 20 cm) sheet pan, base and sides lined with parchment paper

**1** Preheat the oven to 375°F (190°C).

**2** Place all the ingredients for the crumble topping, except the blueberries, in a mixing bowl and rub together with your fingertips until it forms a loose chunky, crumbly mixture. Add the blueberries and mix well, pressing some of them against the side of the bowl so they burst. Put the crumble into the bottom of the pan and press down with the back of a spoon into an even layer.

**3** To make the muffin cake, sift both flours, the salt, and the baking powder into a large bowl. Mix in the ground almonds and set aside.

**4** Cream the butter and sugar for a good 5 minutes in a stand mixer or with an electric hand mixer (or a wooden spoon, if you've got the strength and courage) until pale and fluffy.

**5** Add half of the flour mixture and half of the beaten eggs and whisk for another minute, then add the rest of the flour mixture and eggs with the vanilla paste and beat for a final minute until combined into a smooth cake batter. Fold in the apples and blueberries with a wooden spoon, then spoon the batter into the pan over the crumble and smooth the top.

**6** Bake for 35–45 minutes, or until golden and springy to the touch. Leave the cake to cool completely in the pan, then place a large cutting board over the top and flip it over. Carefully peel off the backing paper to reveal the crumble top.

**7** To make the icing, stir the lemon juice with a splash of water into the powdered sugar until smooth and thick. Drizzle the icing over the cake and serve cut into squares.

Cakes & Desserts

# Blood Orange Olive Oil Cake

I adore blood oranges with their sharp, sweet flavor that reminds me of those little packs of sherbet I had as a kid. They also add a much-needed burst of freshness and color to the start of the year, so when the season comes around I tend to purchase them in abundance. This cake is a celebration of their wonderful flavor, while the olive oil further adds to the taste of the Mediterranean. Obviously, you can make this cake with regular oranges when it's not blood orange season, but I think it's worth the wait!

## Serves 8

3 large eggs
¾ cup (150g) sugar
¾ cup (170g) Greek yogurt
⅔ cup (150ml) extra-virgin olive oil
finely grated zest of 1 blood orange
1 cup (125g) all-purpose flour
1½ tsp baking powder
½ tsp salt
¾ cup (75g) ground almonds

### For the oranges:
4 tbsp sugar
3 blood oranges, thinly sliced, ends discarded (unpeeled)
light brown sugar, for sprinkling

### YOU WILL NEED
8 in (20 cm) round cake pan, base and sides greased and lined with parchment paper

1   To prepare the oranges, heat 1¼ cups (300ml) of water and the sugar in a saucepan until the sugar dissolves. Place the orange slices in the pan (the water should just cover them, but if not add a splash more) and simmer for 25 minutes, until softened. Carefully remove the orange slices and place on a wire cooling rack, with a lined baking tray underneath to catch any drips, to cool completely. Return the pan to medium heat and cook until the liquid reduces by roughly two-thirds and becomes syrupy. Set aside to cool.

2   Preheat the oven to 400°F (200°C).

3   Sprinkle a little brown sugar over the base of the prepared pan and arrange the cooled orange slices on top, overlapping them in a pretty flower spiral pattern.

4   To make the cake, beat the eggs, sugar, yogurt, olive oil, and orange zest with an electric hand mixer or in a stand mixer for about 5 minutes, until light and fluffy. Fold in the flour, baking powder, salt, and ground almonds to make a smooth cake batter. Carefully, pour the cake batter over the orange slices in the base of the cake pan and smooth the top.

5   Bake for 35–40 minutes, or until risen and golden, and a skewer inserted into the middle comes out clean. Leave the cake to cool for 5 minutes in the pan, then carefully turn it out onto a wire rack. Peel off the backing paper and drizzle with the sugar syrup while the cake is still slightly warm. Leave to cool before cutting into slices.

**Cakes & Desserts**

# Salted Caramel Banana Loaf

My stepfather's aunty made the best banana loaf. I know a lot of banana breads, cakes, and loaves were made during lockdown but I doubt they held a candle to Freda's. It's a combination of how easy the cake is to make and the fact that she always used margarine, which gives it that lighter-than-air whipped quality that you simply don't get with butter. I've given it a twist by including a gloriously sticky caramel topping, a good reason to flip it over—it's a joy to behold!

## Serves 10

1⅔ cups (225g) all-purpose
   flour, sifted
2 tsp baking powder
1½ tsp salt
7 tbsp (115g) margarine
½ cup (115g) light brown sugar
1 tsp ground cinnamon
2 ripe bananas, mashed
2 large eggs, beaten

### For the caramel topping:
1¾ cups plus 2 tbsp (175g)
   light brown sugar
1¼ cups (300ml) heavy cream
3 tbsp (50g) salted butter
½ tsp salt
2 firm bananas, to decorate

### YOU WILL NEED
2lb (900g) loaf pan, base and
   sides greased and lined with
   parchment paper

**1** Preheat the oven to 375°F (190°C).

**2** Start with the caramel topping. Combine all the ingredients, except the firm bananas, in a saucepan over low heat, then stir until the sugar dissolves. Turn the heat up slightly and let the sauce bubble away for 2–3 minutes, until golden and syrupy. Set aside.

**3** To make the cake, place the flour, baking powder, salt, margarine, and sugar in a large bowl and mix together with your fingertips to a crumb consistency. Stir in the cinnamon.

**4** Add the mashed ripe bananas and eggs, then beat together with a wooden spoon, to loosen the mixture.

**5** Pour half of the caramel sauce into the lined pan. (Any left over will keep for up to 3 days in an airtight container in the fridge.)

**6** Cut the firm bananas in half lengthwise and place these on top of the caramel, cut-side up, then gently pour in the cake batter and level the top.

**7** Bake for 40 minutes, or until risen and golden, and firm to the touch. Allow the cake to cool in the pan on a wire rack for 15 minutes, then place a plate on top and turn it out to cool completely. Serve cut into slices with extra caramel sauce spooned over, if you like.

**Cakes & Desserts**

# Fruit Gelatin Mold

I grew up in 1970s suburban London where dinner parties were all the rage. My mum's dinner parties were legendary for her fabulous food and, it being the '70s, there was a lot of stuff set in gelatin; if it wasn't fish, it was fruit. I clearly remember sneaking to the top of the stairs to listen in on the guests oohing and aahing at what came out of the kitchen, but the biggest round of applause was when Mum served dessert. This is my take on her gelatin ring. Mum's used to have canned mandarins in it, which are actually my favorite fruit in a can, but I thought I'd attempt something a little more colorful. This may be my new favorite retro-inspired dessert.

## Serves 8

1 tbsp plain gelatin (to make 2¼ cups/600ml)
1 (3oz/85g) package of raspberry gelatin
roughly 1lb 2oz (500g) selection of fruit, such as blueberries, raspberries, and blackberries; chopped peaches or nectarines; halved black grapes; and halved and hulled strawberries
whipped cream, to serve

**YOU WILL NEED**
5-cup (about 2 pint/1.2 liter), tube pan

**1**  Make the plain gelatin and the raspberry gelatin following the instructions on the packets. Mix them together and pour the mixture into a small pitcher or measuring cup.

**2**  Place the fruit in the pan in layers of alternating colors. Really pack in the layers and push them down a little until the pan is completely full.

**3**  Gradually pour the gelatin mixture into the pan—the trick is to fill the pan right up to the top with no gaps. (You may have some of the liquid gelatin left over.) Place the bundt in the fridge and leave the gelatin to chill and set overnight.

**4**  When you're ready to serve, place a platter or cake stand over the pan and carefully flip it over. Remove the pan to reveal the gelatin. If it won't release, pour some hot water into a large pot. Carefully place the bundt pan in the hot water for no more than 5 seconds and then remove and try again. Serve with whipped cream.

**Note:** Do not use kiwi or pineapple. Both contain an enzyme that won't allow the gelatin to set. Learn from my mistakes—believe me it got messy!

# Apple & Honey Bread & Butter Pudding

In my opinion (and my mother's, of course), challah makes the best bread and butter pudding. I think it's the sweet eggy flavor that makes it so much richer and more yummy than regular bread. Apple and honey represent sweetness and are eaten at the Jewish New Year in hope for a sweet year ahead. When buying challah, try to find a lovely Jewish bakery and buy two loaves, one to eat as a regular loaf and one to use for this dessert—after 4 days it will have the perfect level of staleness for a bread and butter pudding.

**Serves 6**

salted butter for spreading, at room temperature
1 loaf of challah bread, thickly sliced (if you can't find challah use brioche)

**For the honey apple custard:**
1¼ cups (300ml) whole milk
1 cup (250ml) heavy cream
2 tsp ground cinnamon
2 large eggs
1 tbsp honey
2 apples, peeled and coarsely grated

**YOU WILL NEED**
9 in (22 cm) fluted pie pan, or similar-size cake or baking pan, greased with butter

**1** Butter both sides of each slice of bread, then cut them into triangles. (I like lots of smaller triangles because the tips become nice and brown in the oven, but this is just my preferred aesthetic styling.) Arrange the buttered triangles randomly in your pan.

**2** To make the custard, gently warm the milk in a saucepan (you want it be steaming but not scalding). Stir in the cream until combined, then add the cinnamon.

**3** In a large bowl, whisk the eggs with the honey for about 3 minutes, until pale and frothy. Pour in half of the warm milk, whisking continuously. Once everything is well mixed, then pour in the rest of the milk and stir well. Stir in the grated apples. Pour the apple custard over the bread and let the whole thing stand for at least 20 minutes.

**4** Meanwhile, preheat the oven to 375°F (190°C).

**5** Bake the bread pudding for 25–35 minutes, or until the custard is bubbling and thick, and the top is golden brown.

**Cakes & Desserts**

# Steamed Syrup Cake

**170**

My husband and I share a birthday, which as you can imagine comes with its own peculiarities. I try to make him a birthday cake each year and, after a lot of trial and error, this one seems to have become written in law. His dessert of choice is steamed syrup pudding—a dense, syrupy steamed cake—a favorite from childhood. This version takes it out of the pudding bowl and into a sheet pan so it's easier to divide up and serve. It's a little bit different, and so wonderfully retro, especially when you see your guests' faces as the cake is put on the table. It makes any effort all the more worthwhile.

**Serves 6–8**

¼ cup (60ml) honey
¼ cup (60ml) molasses
3 tbsp maple syrup
1¾ cups (175g) all-purpose
  flour, sifted
1¾ tsp baking powder
1 tsp baking soda
2 tsp salt
12 tbsp (175g) salted butter,
  softened
4 large eggs
¾ cup (175g) light brown sugar
heavy cream, to serve

**YOU WILL NEED**
10 x 7 in (25 x 18 cm) baking
  pan, base and sides
  greased and lined with
  parchment paper

**1** Preheat the oven to 375°F (190°C). Fill a large roasting pan with water and place it on the bottom shelf of the oven.

**2** In a small bowl, combine the honey, molasses and maple syrup. Drizzle the base of the prepared baking pan liberally with some of the honey mixture (at least 4 tablespoons).

**3** Place the remaining honey mixture with the rest of the ingredients in a large bowl and beat with an electric hand mixer or in a stand mixer until light and smooth. Pour the cake batter into the prepared dish and smooth the top.

**4** Take a sheet of parchment paper that will easily cover your pan and lay a same-size sheet of foil on top, then fold a pleat down the middle of the foil and paper. Place it foil side up over the dish and secure tightly.

**5** Bake on the middle shelf of the oven for 1 hour, then remove the foil and paper covering. Turn the oven down to 350°F (180°C) and bake for another 10–15 minutes, until risen and golden. Check to make sure the cake is firm to the touch; if not, place it back in the oven for a few more minutes. Leave the cake in the pan for about 20 minutes before placing a platter on top and flipping it over. Carefully peel off the backing paper before cutting the cake into squares. Serve with cream.

**Cakes & Desserts**

# Aperol, Apricot, & Peach Cobbler

Back in my marketing days Aperol was one of our clients. Not only is it a fabulous summery aperitivo but the people behind the brand were the loveliest to work with and we had a lot of fun promoting the drink. I still seem to have a surplus of it in numerous cupboards dotted throughout the house and my over-consumption during those days means I don't drink it as much now, so I've had to find other uses. Aperol works well combined with summer fruit, as its slight bitterness cuts through the sweetness—this cobbler is a divine example. If preferred, you could sub out the Aperol for orange juice mixed with a teaspoon of bitters for a similar vibe.

## Serves 6

6 apricots, stones removed, cut into quarters
3 peaches, stones removed, cut into quarters
4 tbsp Aperol
1 tsp lemon thyme
1 tbsp honey (more if you have a sweet tooth)
whipped cream or ice cream, to serve

### For the cobbler:
¾ cup (100g) all-purpose flour
1 tsp baking powder
½ tsp salt
½ cup (50g) ground almonds
¼ cup (50g) sugar
3 tbsp (50g) cold salted butter, cut into small cubes
1 egg, beaten
2 tbsp whole milk

### YOU WILL NEED
10 x 6 in (25 x 15 cm) baking pan, base and sides greased and lined with parchment paper

**1** Preheat the oven to 400°F (200°C).

**2** Place the fruit, Aperol, lemon thyme, and honey in a large bowl and stir well. Set aside while you make the cobbler dough.

**3** Mix the flour, baking powder, salt, ground almonds, and sugar in a large bowl. Add the butter and rub everything together with your fingertips until it forms a breadcrumb texture. Add the egg and milk and, with your hand shaped like a claw, bring everything together to form a dough. It will be relatively wet, like a loose scone mix.

**4** Place large dollops of the cobbler dough in the bottom of the baking pan. You can be neat and tidy about this, but I prefer random dollops with gaps. Spoon the fruit mixture onto the cobbler base.

**5** Bake for 35–40 minutes, until everything is bubbling and the cobbler has risen and pushed between some of the fruit. Remove from the oven and leave to cool. Serve the cobbler as it is with whipped cream or ice cream or be really brave and place a large platter on top and flip it over. Carefully, peel off the backing paper to reveal the cobbler top.

# Summer Berry Bread Pudding

I absolutely adore the combination of cold cooked fruit with cream. I think it's the blend of tart sweetness with the rich silkiness that really makes me happy. Then encase the fruity goodness in juice-soaked bread and you have a winner of a dessert that is ridiculously easy to make, even if flipping it the right way up can be a bit of a workout! The Campari adds a touch of tipsy elegance to the proceedings and elevates this humble pudding to a classier dessert.

## Serves 6

1lb 8oz (700g) frozen mixed berries
3½oz (100g) fresh or frozen blackberries
¾ cup (150g) sugar
4 tbsp Campari (optional but certainly delicious) or marmalade
8–10 slices of medium-thick white bread from a large loaf, crusts removed
heavy cream, to serve

### YOU WILL NEED

1¾-pint (1-liter) ovenproof bowl, lightly brushed with vegetable oil (or line with plastic wrap if you prefer a stress-free reveal, but I like living dangerously)

1. Place all the berries (no need to defrost them first) in a large saucepan with the sugar and Campari or marmalade. Cook over medium heat, stirring occasionally, for 3–5 minutes, until the sugar dissolves and the juices begin to run, then remove the pan from the heat.

2. Cut 1 slice of the bread into a round to fit the base of the pudding basin. Cut 4 slices in half and use them to line the sides of the basin, overlapping the straight edges and with the rounded-side down, pressing the edges together to seal. Fill any gaps with small pieces of bread, to prevent any juices seeping out when you add the fruit.

3. Pour in the fruit and any juices, saving a cupful, then cover the top of the pudding with the remaining bread. Place a small plate or saucer, one that fits exactly inside the rim of the bowl, on top. Place a weight on top (an old scale weight would work, or a bag of rice) and leave in the fridge overnight.

4. Just before serving, loosen the chilled pudding using a palette knife, and then place a larger plate or bowl on top and flip it right-side up. A couple of taps on the top should loosen the pudding nicely. Remove the basin, then spoon the reserved fruit and juices all over, to soak any bits of bread that still look white (a pastry brush is useful here). Serve cut into wedges with lots of cold cream.

**Cakes & Desserts**

# Grandma Jennie's Ginger Loaf Cake

This cake takes me back to lovelier times. It was my grandma Jennie's recipe, who passed it down to Mum, who has since given it to me. It's utterly delightful. Soft, sweet, and light with a bit of a kick from the crystallized ginger. It's also dairy-free, which is another bonus.

## Serves 10

3 tbsp (50g) crystallized ginger, cut into small pieces
2 large eggs
1 cup (200g) sugar
3 tbsp honey
¾ cup (175ml) sunflower oil
½ tsp baking soda mixed in ½ cup (120ml) of warm water
2 cups (250g) all-purpose flour, sifted
2½ tsp baking powder
1½ tsp salt
4 tsp ground ginger
1 tsp ground cinnamon

### YOU WILL NEED
2lb (900g) loaf pan, base and sides greased and lined with parchment paper

1 Preheat the oven to 375°F (190°C).

2 Sprinkle the crystallized ginger into the base of the loaf pan and spread it out evenly—you should have a thin, knobbly layer of ginger. Set aside.

3 In a large bowl, whisk the eggs and sugar with an electric hand mixer or in a stand mixer until pale and doubled in volume. Mix in the honey, followed by the sunflower oil and baking soda and water mix.

4 Fold in the flour, baking powder, salt, and spices to make a very loose cake batter; this is how it should be. Pour the batter carefully into the loaf pan and level the top.

5 Bake for 45 minutes but check after 40 minutes—if it's getting too dark, turn the heat down to 350°F (170°C), or place some foil over the top to stop it from burning. The cake is ready when risen and golden, and a skewer or knife inserted into the middle comes out clean. Leave it to cool completely in the pan on a wire rack before turning it out and cutting into slices to serve.

**Cakes & Desserts**

# Sweet Tarts of Joy

When we were kids, Mum always encouraged my brother and I to learn and love cooking. We would sit and watch her in the kitchen, where she allowed us to stir ingredients together and, of course, we always fought over who got to lick the spoon. One of the most simple and joyful things we did was fill little pastry cases to make sticky jam tarts. As we grew up, Mum taught me more complex dishes (my brother was no doubt outside playing while I preferred to be in the kitchen). But even those dishes were pretty easy. She would often simply mix fresh fruit in a bowl with a touch of sugar, then spoon it into a pie crust before baking. It has always fascinated me how such incredible dishes could come from just a handful of everyday ingredients, and it's these simple pleasures that I want to share with you in this final chapter.

# Pineapple Puffs

In the 17th century, the pineapple was a symbol of wealth, luxury, and hospitality in the UK. Seen as such an honor to serve it at home, people would rent a whole fruit to sit in the middle of the dining table just to impress guests. Fast forward 300 years to the mid-twentieth century when the pineapple was still impressing people but this time in upside-down cake form, which has since become a classic. These pineapple puffs are so unbelievably quick and easy to make. They're also ridiculously delicious, and with just a handful of ingredients you have a joyful dessert.

## Makes 6

2 premade 9¾ x 10½ in sheets of puff pastry or use homemade (see p.12) rolled to 14 x 9 in (35 x 23 cm)
drizzle of honey
6 canned pineapple rings
6 Maraschino cherries
1 egg, beaten
powdered sugar, for dusting (optional)

### YOU WILL NEED
large sheet pan, roughly 15 x 10½ in (38 x 27 cm), lined with parchment paper
4-in (10-cm) cookie cutter, ramekin, or bowl

**1** Preheat the oven to 425°F (220°C). Remove the pastry from the fridge and set aside.

**2** Using the 4-in (10-cm) cookie cutter, ramekin, or bowl as a template, draw 6 disks onto the parchment paper, leaving space between each one. Place the parchment paper back on the pan, drawn side down. Drizzle honey on the drawn disks, then lay a pineapple ring on top. Place a cherry in the center of each ring.

**3** Lay out the puff pastry and, using the same cookie cutter, cut out 6 disks. (Save any leftover pastry to use in another recipe, see pp.14–15.) Lay a pastry disk over each pineapple ring. Using the back of a fork, press indentations around the edge of the pastry to seal. Score a cross diagonally over the top of each one with a sharp knife and then brush with egg.

**4** Bake for 10 minutes, then turn the oven down to 375°F (190°C) and cook for a further 20 minutes, until the pastry is golden and puffy. Remove from the oven and allow the tarts to sit on the pan for 5 minutes before flipping them over with a spatula. Dust with powdered sugar, if you like, and serve.

**Sweet Tarts of Joy**

# Hot & Cold Eton Mess Tart

A much-loved dessert in the UK, the Eton mess originated, as the name suggests, at Eton College, where it is said a pavlova of berries, cream, and meringue was accidentally dropped and then simply scooped up and served jumbled together. I love this style of thinking and cooking, and so I've re-created an upside-down version—I'm so glad I did!

**Serves 6**

2 premade 9¾ x 10½ in sheets of puff pastry or use homemade (see p.12) rolled to 14 x 9 in (35 x 23 cm)
3 tbsp strawberry jam
1 egg, beaten
drizzle of honey
3½oz (100g) blueberries, plus extra to decorate
3½oz (100g) blackberries, plus extra to decorate
4 premade 4-in (10-cm) meringues, broken into chunks
roughly 5 scoops of vanilla ice cream
1¼ cups (300ml) heavy cream, whipped, to serve

**For the coulis:**
7oz (200g) strawberries, hulled, plus extra to serve
1 tbsp sugar

**YOU WILL NEED**
2 large sheet pans, roughly 15 x 10½ in (38 x 27 cm), lined with parchment paper

**1** Preheat the oven to 425°F (220°C). Remove the pastry from the fridge and set aside.

**2** First make the coulis. Place half of the strawberries in a blender with the sugar and blitz to a rough purée. Set aside.

**3** Roll out the puff pastry and slather one side with the strawberry jam, leaving a ½-in (1-cm) border all the way round. Flip it over and place the pastry, jam side down, on one of the lined sheet pans. Score the top in a diamond pattern with a sharp knife and then brush with egg. Bake for 25 minutes, until risen and golden.

**4** While the pastry is baking, mark out a 14 x 9 in (35 x 23 cm) rectangle on the second sheet of parchment paper and place it drawn side down on the second sheet pan. Drizzle with a little honey.

**5** Leaving a ½-in (1-cm) border, start to layer half of the blueberries, blackberries, and strawberries. Drizzle with a third of the strawberry coulis and top with half of the broken meringues. Place scoops of vanilla ice cream on top and then repeat with a second layer of berries, strawberry coulis, and meringue. Don't worry, it's supposed to look messy! Place the pan in the freezer until the fruit mixture is just firm.

**6** Once baked, flip the pastry over and carefully peel off the backing paper. Leave the pastry to cool slightly while you remove the pan from the freezer.

**7** Gently lay the cooked puff pastry, jam-side down, on top of the frozen berry mess, then lay a piece of parchment paper on top, followed by a cutting board or platter. Flip the whole thing over and peel off the backing paper to reveal the top. Dress the top with fresh whipped cream, more berries, and the remaining strawberry coulis drizzled over.

**Sweet Tarts of Joy**

# Cherry Bakewell Tart

**184**

Growing up, I remember Mum buying us boxes of cherry Bakewell slices. Dainty and delicate, and oh so sweet! They were the only treats she allowed in the house, knowing that if she bought others they would be found by my brother and I and eaten in seconds, but the cherry Bakewell slices were special. There was something very grown-up about the almond filling. We always felt so posh eating them, and I wanted to re-create the cakes as an upside-down treat.

**Serves 8**

2 premade 9¾ x 10½ in sheets of puff pastry or use homemade (see p.12) rolled to 14 x 9 in (35 x 23 cm)
drizzle of honey
½ cup (50g) flaked almonds, toasted
roughly 12 black cherries, cut in half and pitted
2 tbsp cherry or raspberry jam
1 egg, beaten
powdered sugar, for dusting (optional)

**For the frangipane:**
½ cup (125g) salted butter, softened
½ cup plus 3 tbsp (125g) sugar
2 large eggs, beaten
1¼ cups (125g) ground almonds
3 drops of almond extract

**YOU WILL NEED**
large sheet pan, roughly 15 x 10½ in (38 x 27 cm), lined with parchment paper
8½-in (22-cm) round plate (it needs to fit on the pastry)

1  Preheat the oven to 425°F (220°C). Remove the pastry from the fridge and set aside.

2  Start with making the frangipane. Using an electric hand mixer, cream the butter and sugar in a large mixing bowl for about 3 minutes, until pale and fluffy. Add the eggs and half of the ground almonds and beat again until combined. Mix in the almond extract and the rest of the ground almonds until everything is well incorporated, then set aside.

3  Draw around the 8½-in (22-cm) plate onto the parchment paper, then place it drawn side down on the sheet pan. Drizzle with a little honey and sprinkle with the flaked almonds.

4  Leaving a ½-in (1-cm) border, arrange the cherry halves on top of the drawn circle, packing them close together (this can be done quite haphazardly or neatly, as you prefer). Spoon the frangipane on and carefully spread it out in an even layer.

5  Roll out the puff pastry and, using the same plate as before, cut around it to make a disk. Slather the jam on one side of the pastry, leaving a narrow border around the edge. Lay the puff pastry, jam side down, over the top of the frangipane. Using the back of a fork, press indentations around the edge of the pastry to seal. Score the top in a diamond pattern with a sharp knife and then brush with egg.

6  Bake for 30 minutes, or until the pastry is wonderfully golden and puffy. Remove from the oven and allow the tart to sit on the pan for 15 minutes. Lay a piece of parchment paper on top, followed by a cutting board or plate, and carefully flip the tart over. Peel off the backing paper. Dust the top with powdered sugar, if you like, and cut into wedges to serve.

**Sweet Tarts of Joy**

# Apple & Berry Compote Lattice Pie

As I mentioned earlier in the book, autumn is my favorite time of the year. Yes, it means cooler, shorter days but it also brings the promise of cozy fireside evenings, crisp brisk walks over golden leaves, and the thought that Christmas is not too far away. A lattice apple pie does that for me too—autumn's harvest wrapped in pastry. Utterly divine! This one is slightly fiddly as you weave the pastry strips into a lattice pattern, but with a little practice it can be quite therapeutic.

## Serves 4–6

2 recipes of homemade pie dough (see p.13) each rolled out to roughly 14 x 9 in (35 x 23 cm)
6 tbsp (100g) salted butter, melted
2 tbsp sugar
3 apples, peeled, cored and cut into very small dice
3 tbsp homemade berry compote or mixed berry jam
1 egg, beaten
powdered sugar, for dusting (optional)

### YOU WILL NEED

large sheet pan, roughly 15 x 10½ in (38 x 27 cm), lined with parchment paper

1  Preheat the oven to 425°F (220°C). Unroll one sheet of the pie dough, placing it vertically in front of you, and cut into ¾-in- (2-cm-) wide strips. Lay them out on a pan and pop it in the fridge.

2  Mark out a 14 x 9 in (35 x 23 cm) rectangle on the parchment paper and place it drawn side down on the sheet pan. Brush with the melted butter and sprinkle with the sugar.

3  Lay half of the strips of pie dough vertically over the drawn rectangle (it doesn't matter if they go slightly over the line because they are trimmed later) and then weave the remaining strips diagonally over and under to create an open-lattice pattern.

4  Place the apples in a bowl, add the compote or jam and mix well, then dump the mixture onto the pastry lattice in a rough rectangular heap in the middle. Gently spread out the apple mixture, leaving a ¾-in (2-cm) border around the edge.

5  Roll out the second sheet of pie dough and drape it over the apple mixture. Trim the edges of the pie, if needed, to neaten. Using the back of a spoon or fork, press indentations around the edge of the pastry to seal. Score the top in a diamond pattern with a sharp knife and then brush with egg.

6  Bake for 30–35 minutes, until the pastry is golden and crisp. Remove from the oven and allow the pie to sit on the pan for 5 minutes. Lay a piece of parchment paper on top, followed by a cutting board, and carefully flip the pie over. Peel off the backing paper. Dust the top with powdered sugar, if you like, before serving.

**Sweet Tarts of Joy**

# Banana, Toffee, & Cream Cheese Tarts

The thing I love about my upside-down recipes is that while I have an idea in my head about how they are going to turn out, sometimes the result is quite different. More often than I'd like to admit, it's a disaster and the tart needs reworking, but at other times it's a brilliant accidental mistake. These tarts started out as simply banana and honey, but magically they turned to toffee in the oven. Banoffee is a perennial favorite flavor, and combining it with a beautiful salted cream cheese will blow your mind.

## Makes 2

2 premade 9¾ x 10½ in sheets of puff pastry or use homemade (see p.12) rolled to 14 x 9 in (35 x 23 cm)
6 tbsp (100g) salted butter, melted
drizzle of honey
2 tbsp light brown sugar
3 firm bananas, peeled
2 tbsp cream cheese
½ tsp salt
1 egg, beaten
vanilla ice cream, to serve (optional)

### YOU WILL NEED
large sheet pan, roughly 15 x 10½ in (38 x 27 cm), lined with parchment paper

1 Preheat the oven to 425°F (220°C). Remove the pastry from the fridge and set aside.

2 Mark out 2 rectangles on the sheet of parchment paper, roughly 6½ x 9 in (17 x 23 cm), leaving space between each one. Place the parchment paper back on the pan, drawn side down. Brush each rectangle with the melted butter, then drizzle with a little honey and sprinkle with the brown sugar.

3 Cut the bananas in half lengthwise and lay them, cut side down, on the buttery sugar mixture. Use 3 banana halves per tart and arrange them in the middle of the rectangles, leaving a border.

4 Roll out the puff pastry and cut it in half to make 2 rectangles the same size as the ones drawn on the parchment paper. Slather the cream cheese on one side of each pastry rectangle, leaving a ½-in (1-cm) border around the edge. Sprinkle with the salt. Lay the pastry, cheese side down, over the bananas. Using the back of a fork, press indentations around the edge of the pastry to seal. Score the top of each one in a diamond pattern with a sharp knife and then brush with egg.

5 Bake for 30 minutes, or until the pastry is wonderfully golden and puffy. Remove from the oven and allow the tarts to sit on the pan for 5 minutes. Lay a piece of parchment paper on top, followed by a cutting board, and carefully flip the tarts over. Peel off the backing paper. Serve topped with scoops of vanilla ice cream, if you like.

# Herringbone Rhubarb Tart

If the truth be told, I'm not a fancy cake decorator or a food stylist for that matter. I have big-man syndrome when it comes to being delicate with cake and pastry craft, and I lack that dainty touch. This is why I prefer to keep things simple. However, if the moment grabs me and I have a clear head, I get creative—and this herringbone rhubarb tart is worth being patient for.

**Serves 6**

2 premade 9¾ x 10½ in sheets of puff pastry or use homemade (see p.12) rolled to 14 x 9 in (35 x 23 cm)
drizzle of honey
roughly 8 rhubarb stalks (try to use ones of a similar thickness), each cut into 2-in- (5-cm-) long pieces
2 tbsp sugar
1 egg, beaten
whipped cream, to serve (optional)

**YOU WILL NEED**
large sheet pan, roughly 15 x 10½ in (38 x 27 cm), lined with parchment paper

1 Preheat the oven to 350°F (180°C). Remove the pastry from the fridge and set aside.

2 Mark out a 14 x 9 in (35 x 23 cm) rectangle on the parchment paper and place it drawn side down on the sheet pan. Drizzle with the honey.

3 Leaving a ½-in (1-cm) border, lay the pieces of rhubarb on top of the drawn rectangle in a herringbone pattern. With the sheet pan placed horizontally in front of you, start at the top left-hand corner and work downward in a row, placing the pieces of rhubarb on a diagonal. Return to the top and create a second row, laying the rhubarb diagonally in the opposite direction in a chevron pattern. Continue until you have used all the fruit and have a herringbone pattern. Trim the edges of the rhubarb to neaten and sprinkle with the sugar.

4 Roll out the puff pastry and place it over the rhubarb. Using the back of a fork, press indentations around the edge of the pastry to seal. Score the top in a diamond pattern with a sharp knife and then brush with egg.

5 Bake for 35 minutes, or until the pastry is wonderfully golden and puffy. Remove from the oven and allow the tart to sit on the pan for 5 minutes. There will be some glorious liquid released from the cooked rhubarb sitting in the pan. Carefully tilt the pan and pour the juices into a pitcher or measuring cup. Once the liquid is poured off, lay a piece of parchment paper on top of the tart, followed by a cutting board, and carefully flip it over. Peel off the backing paper, then pour the liquid over the rhubarb. Serve with whipped cream, if you like.

**Sweet Tarts of Joy**

# Pear & Chocolate Tarts

This combination of ingredients always reminds me of my first trip to Paris. While the city is stunning, I was more fascinated by the incredible cafés and patisseries, as you can imagine. The use of chocolate with fruit always seemed a little odd to me until I tried the most sensational pear and chocolate tart in a Parisian cafe, and I have been forever hooked.

## Makes 2

2 premade 9¾ x 10½ in sheets of puff pastry or use homemade (see p.12) rolled to 14 x 9 in (35 x 23 cm)
drizzle of honey
1 tbsp sugar
handful of toasted slivered almonds
2 firm pears, cored and thickly sliced (unpeeled)
3½oz (100g) 70% dark chocolate, finely chopped
1 egg, beaten

### YOU WILL NEED
large sheet pan, roughly 15 x 10½ in (38 x 27 cm), lined with parchment paper

1  Preheat the oven to 425°F (220°C). Remove the pastry from the fridge and set aside.

2  Mark out 2 rectangles on the sheet of parchment paper, roughly 6½ x 9 in (17 x 23 cm), leaving space between each one. Place the parchment paper back on the pan, drawn side down. Drizzle with a little honey, then sprinkle with the sugar and slivered almonds.

3  Leaving a ½-in (1-cm) border, lay half of the sliced pears on top of each of the rectangles, then sprinkle with the chocolate.

4  Roll out the puff pastry and cut it to make 2 rectangles the same size as the ones drawn on the parchment paper. Lay the pastry pieces over the pears and chocolate. Using your fingers, press down the edges of the pastry to seal. Score the top of each one in a diamond pattern with a sharp knife and then brush with egg.

5  Bake for 25 minutes, until the pastry is wonderfully golden and puffy. Remove from the oven and allow the tarts to sit on the pan for 5 minutes. Lay a piece of parchment paper on top, followed by a cutting board, and carefully flip the tarts over. Peel off the backing paper before serving.

**Sweet Tarts of Joy**

# Mango, Rum, & Coconut Tarts

One of my favorite aromas in the world is the blend of Hawaiian Tropic sunscreen with cigarette smoke. I know—this is wrong on so many levels but it takes me back to childhood trips to Spain and the fabulous old ladies laid out on the beach with their baked-on suntans, sun hats, chiffon caftans, and long painted nails gripped around a smoking cigarette. These mango and coconut tarts capture the essence of the tropics, and they also happen to be equally beautifully bronzed!

**195**

## Makes 6

1 recipe of homemade pie dough (see p.13) rolled out to roughly 14 x 9 in (35 x 23 cm)
1 large ripe mango, peeled, stone removed, and finely chopped, divided
3 tbsp honey
2 tbsp dark spiced rum
3 tbsp coconut flakes, plus extra, toasted, to decorate
3 tbsp (50g) salted butter, melted, divided
juice and finely grated zest of ½ lime
1 egg, beaten

### YOU WILL NEED
large sheet pan, roughly 15 x 10½ in (38 x 27 cm), lined with parchment paper
4-in (10-cm) cookie cutter, ramekin, or bowl

**1** Preheat the oven to 350°F (180°C). Remove the pie dough from the fridge and set aside.

**2** Put half of the mango, the honey, the rum, the coconut, and two-thirds of the melted butter in a large bowl. Add the lime juice and mix well until combined. Set aside.

**3** Using the 4-in (10-cm) cookie cutter, ramekin, or bowl as a template, draw 6 disks onto the parchment paper, leaving space between each one. Place the parchment paper back on the sheet pan, drawn side down.

**4** Leaving a ½-in (1-cm) border, place a tablespoonful of the mango mixture in the center of each disk. Brush the parchment paper around each pile of mango with a little melted butter.

**5** Roll out the pie dough and, using the same cookie cutter, cut out 6 disks. (Save any leftover pastry to use in another recipe, see pp.14–15.) Lay a pastry disk over each pile of mango. Using the back of a fork, press indentations around the edge of the pastry to seal. Score the top of each one in a diamond pattern with a sharp knife and then brush with egg.

**6** Bake for 35 minutes, until the pastry is darkly golden. Remove from the oven and allow the tarts to sit on the pan for 5 minutes before flipping them over with a spatula. Spoon the remaining mango on top of each tart and sprinkle with the toasted coconut and lime zest.

**Sweet Tarts of Joy**

# Citrus & Pistachio Frangipane Tart

196

This is what I'd call a proper fancy tart, although it's really quite simple to make. Pistachios add a flavor twist to the frangipane, and when the tart is flipped over, the contrast of the ombré citrus fruit and the pale green of the nuts is really quite pretty. This tart needs to be made during the blood orange season, but if you can't find any, then a small pink grapefruit would work just as well.

**Serves 6**

1 recipe of homemade pie
   dough (see p.13) rolled out
   to roughly 14 x 9 in
   (35 x 23 cm)
drizzle of honey
1 unwaxed lemon, finely sliced
   and ends discarded
   (unpeeled)
1 orange, finely sliced and ends
   discarded (unpeeled)
1 blood orange, finely sliced
   and ends discarded
   (unpeeled)
1 egg, beaten

### For the pistachio frangipane:

1 cup (140g) shelled pistachios
½ cup (100g) sugar
finely grated zest of
   1 unwaxed lemon
6 tbsp (100g) salted butter,
   cut into cubes
2 eggs
½ cup (75g) all-purpose flour

### YOU WILL NEED

large sheet pan, roughly
   15 x 10½ in (38 x 27 cm),
   lined with parchment paper

1. Preheat the oven to 350°F (180°C). Remove the pastry from the fridge and set aside.

2. First make the frangipane. Blitz the pistachios, sugar, and lemon zest in a food processor to a fine, sand-like crumb. In a mixing bowl, beat the butter using an electric hand mixer until creamy. Add the eggs, flour, and the pistachio mixture and beat again until thick. Set aside.

3. Mark out a 14 x 9 in (35 x 23 cm) rectangle on the parchment paper and place it drawn side down on the sheet pan. Place the lined sheet pan vertically on the worktop and drizzle with a little honey.

4. Leaving a ½-in (1-cm) border, lay the slices of citrus fruit on top of the drawn rectangle, starting with two rows of lemon, then orange, and finally blood orange to create an ombré effect. Slather the frangipane on top, taking care not to disrupt the layer of fruit.

5. Roll out the pie dough and lay it on top of the frangipane and fruit. Using the back of a fork, press indentations around the edge of the pastry to seal. Score the top in a diamond pattern with a sharp knife and then brush with egg.

6. Bake for 35 minutes, or until the pastry is wonderfully golden and crisp. Remove from the oven and allow the tart to sit on the pan for 5 minutes. Lay a piece of parchment paper on top, followed by a cutting board or plate, and carefully flip the tart over. Peel off the backing paper before serving.

**Sweet Tarts of Joy**

# Plum & Pear Cobbler Tart

At the end of the summer, edging into autumn in the UK, the Victoria plum trees are laden with fruit. You have to be quick to pick them before the wasps get wind of their ripeness, but if you do you will eat the kind of plums that remind me of my childhood. Pears are also beginning to ripen at this time of year, and so this tart is a homage to my favorite season.

## Serves 6

1 recipe of homemade pie dough (see p.13) rolled out to roughly 14 x 9 in (35 x 23 cm)
drizzle of honey
4 Victoria plums, or other type of plum, stones removed, and cut into quarters
2 pears, cut into quarters and core removed (unpeeled)
1 tsp fennel seeds
1 egg, beaten
vanilla ice cream, to serve (optional)

### For the cobbler topping:
¾ cup (100g) all-purpose flour, sifted
1 tsp baking powder
¾ tsp salt
½ cup (50g) ground almonds
3 tbsp (50g) cold salted butter, cut into cubes
¼ cup (50g) sugar
1 egg, beaten
2 tbsp whole milk

### YOU WILL NEED
large sheet pan, roughly 15 x 10½ in (38 x 27 cm), lined with parchment paper

1 Preheat the oven to 425°F (220°C). Remove the pastry from the fridge and set aside.

2 First make the cobbler topping. Place all the ingredients in a large bowl and rub together with your fingertips or beat with an electric hand mixer. It should have the consistency of a loose scone dough. Set aside.

3 Mark out a 14 x 9 in (35 x 23 cm) rectangle on the parchment paper and place it drawn side down on the sheet pan. Drizzle with a little honey.

4 Leaving a ¾-in (2-cm) border, spoon the cobbler mixture on top of the drawn rectangle. I like to dollop the cobbler in a rough pattern but you can place it in one neat layer, if you prefer. Lay the plums and pears on top of the cobbler dough in a random way, squishing some into the cobbler. Sprinkle the fennel seeds evenly on top.

5 Roll out the pie dough and lay it over the fruit and cobbler. Using the back of a fork, press indentations around the edge of the pastry to seal. Score the top in a diamond pattern with a sharp knife and then brush with egg.

6 Bake for 35–40 minutes, or until the pastry is wonderfully golden and crisp. Remove from the oven and allow the tart to sit on the pan for 5 minutes. Lay a piece of parchment paper on top, followed by a cutting board or plate, and carefully flip the tart over. Peel off the backing paper. Serve the tart with vanilla ice cream, if you like.

**Sweet Tarts of Joy**

# Christmas Pudding Brownie Pie

I thought I'd leave one of the best till last, and this stunning pie is a love letter to the much-loved festive season. It's a wonderful way to use up any bits of leftover Christmas pudding you may have, but it also works really well with Christmas cake or any kind of rich fruit cake. It's a final indulgence for that week between Christmas and New Year when calories don't really matter!

**Serves 6**

2 premade 9¾ x 10½ in sheets of puff pastry or use homemade (see p.12) rolled to 14 x 9 in (35 x 23 cm)
3 tbsp (50g) salted butter, melted
3½oz (100g) leftover Christmas pudding (or fruitcake or date cake)
1 egg, beaten
powdered sugar, for dusting
whipped brandy cream, to serve

**For the brownie:**
8 tbsp (120g) salted butter
4oz (120g) good-quality 70% dark chocolate, broken into squares
2 large eggs
1 cup (200g) sugar
⅔ cup (80g) all-purpose flour, sifted
pinch of salt
4 tsp cocoa powder, sifted

**YOU WILL NEED**
large sheet pan, roughly 15 x 10½ in (38 x 27 cm), lined with parchment paper

1  Preheat the oven to 425°F (220°C). Remove the pastry from the fridge and set aside.

2  Mark out a 14 x 9 in (35 x 23 cm) rectangle on the parchment paper and place it drawn side down on the sheet pan. Brush the drawn rectangle with the melted butter.

3  Leaving a ¾-in (2-cm) border, crumble half of the leftover Christmas pudding over the butter. You want fairly large crumbs, they shouldn't be too fine.

4  To make the brownie, gently melt the butter and chocolate in a saucepan over very low heat, stirring regularly. Take the pan off the heat before the chocolate fully melts and stir occasionally until melted. Set aside to cool slightly.

5  In a large bowl, beat the egg and sugar with an electric hand mixer for about 6 minutes, until doubled in volume and pale, light, and airy. Gently fold in the chocolate mixture until fully combined, then fold in the flour, salt, and cocoa powder. Once combined, carefully spoon the brownie mix over the crumbled pudding on the lined sheet pan. It is quite a thick cake batter and shouldn't run too much. Crumble the remaining Christmas pudding on top.

6  Roll out the puff pastry and lay it over the top of the brownie mixture. Using the back of a fork, press indentations around the edge of the pastry to seal. Score the top in a diamond pattern with a sharp knife and then brush with egg.

7  Bake for 25–30 minutes, or until the pastry is wonderfully golden and puffy. Remove from the oven and allow the pie to sit on the pan for 5 minutes. Lay a piece of parchment paper on top, followed by a cutting board or plate, and carefully flip the pie over. Peel off the backing paper and leave the pie to cool before dusting with powdered sugar. Serve with brandy cream.

*Sweet Tarts of Joy*

# Index

## A

almonds
  Aperol, apricot, & peach cobbler 173
  apricot, polenta, & almond cake 155
  blueberry & apple muffin cake 161
  cherry Bakewell tart 184
  pear & chocolate tarts 192
  plum & pear cobbler tart 198
Aperol, apricot, & peach cobbler 173
apples
  apple & berry compote lattice pie 187
  apple & honey bread & butter
    pudding 168
  blueberry & apple muffin cake 161
apricots
  Aperol, apricot, & peach cobbler 173
  apricot, polenta, & almond cake 155
asparagus
  leftover veggie slaw with mint, pea,
    & cottage cheese dressing 112
  summer veggie lasagna 137
  sun-dried tomato pesto, sausage,
    & cauliflower bake 128
  zucchini, asparagus, & eggplant
    parmigiana 132
arugula: warm caprese salad with
  roasted tomato vinaigrette 109
asparagus & Ibérico ham tarts 28
avocados
  Brussels sprout Caesar salad 121
  chopped salad with smoked chili-fried
    chickpeas 110
  warm caprese salad with roasted
    tomato vinaigrette 109

## B

bacon
  chili shrimp, honey, & bacon
    canapés 82
  full English breakfast pie 53
  St. Patrick's day bacon & colcannon
    pie 92
bananas
  banana, coffee, & cinnamon
    cake 158
  banana, toffee, & cream cheese
    tarts 188
  salted caramel banana loaf 164
beans
  burrito pie 72
  chili non-carne casserole 125
  full English breakfast pie 53
  marmalade & blood orange chicken
    bake 149
  roasted potato, beef, & bean hot pot
    146
  sausage, tomato & bean tarts 31
  sun-dried tomato pesto, sausage,
    & cauliflower bake 128
  veggie sausage, shallot, & bean
    tagliatelle bake 134

beef
  burrito pie 72
  roasted potato, beef, & bean hot pot
    146
  upside down Cornish pasties 44
beets
  beet, red onion, & goat cheese tart 48
  marmalade & blood orange chicken
    bake 149
  sausage cobbler 150
blackberries
  hot & cold Eton mess tart 182
  summer berry bread pudding 174
blood orange olive oil cake 162
blueberries
  blueberry & apple muffin cake 161
  hot & cold Eton mess tart 182
bread
  apple & honey bread & butter
    pudding 168
  Brussels sprout Caesar salad 121
  chicken parm pie 65
  fattoushanella salad 118
  feta, tomato, & strawberry panzanella
    salad 116
  summer berry bread pudding 174
  tumbet savory crumble 140
Brussels sprout Caesar salad 121
Burns Night Cullen skink canapés 88
burrito pie 72

## C

cabbage
  leftover veggie slaw with mint, pea,
    & cottage cheese dressing 112
  roasted potato, beef, & bean hot pot
    146
  St. Patrick's day bacon & colcannon
    pie 92
cakes
  apricot, polenta, & almond cake 155
  banana, coffee, & cinnamon
    cake 158
  blood orange olive oil cake 162
  blueberry & apple muffin cake 161
  Grandma Jennie's ginger loaf
    cake 176
  pineapple & rum cake 156
  salted caramel banana loaf 164
canapés
  Burns Night Cullen skink 88
  chili shrimp, honey, & bacon 82
  garlic mushroom & rosemary
    "vol au vents" 86
  New Year's Eve ham & Stilton 85
  smoked salmon & cream cheese 98
capers
  Brussels sprout Caesar salad 121
  tartar sauce 17
carrots
  carrot, cilantro, & feta tarts 41
  chicken pot pie 50

chicken thigh risotto 126
chili non-carne casserole 125
last of the summer veggie stew
  & dumplings 143
leftover veggie slaw with mint, pea,
  & cottage cheese dressing 112
marmalade & blood orange chicken
  bake 149
potato, carrot, & onion kugel 103
roast in the hole 144
roasted potato, beef, & bean hot pot
  146
sausage cobbler 150
sun-dried tomato pesto, sausage,
  & cauliflower bake 128
upside down vegetable samosas 37
cauliflower
  leftover veggie slaw with mint, pea,
    & cottage cheese dressing 112
  sun-dried tomato pesto, sausage,
    & cauliflower bake 128
celery
  chicken pot pie 50
  chicken thigh risotto 126
  chili non-carne casserole 125
  leftover veggie slaw with mint, pea,
    & cottage cheese dressing 112
  roast in the hole 144
  roasted potato, beef, & bean hot pot
    146
  sausage cobbler 150
  tuna melt tarts 21
cheese
  asparagus & Ibérico ham tarts 28
  beet, red onion, & goat cheese tart 48
  Brussels sprout Caesar salad 121
  Burns Night Cullen skink canapés 88
  burrito pie 72
  carrot, cilantro, & feta tarts 41
  cheesy leek tart 62
  cheesy potato tarts 25
  cherry tomato, nettle, & mozzarella
    phyllo tart 68
  chicken parm pie 65
  chili non-carne casserole 125
  chopped salad with smoked
    chili-fried chickpeas 110
  fattoushanella salad 118
  feta, tomato, & strawberry panzanella
    salad 116
  French onion soup tarte tatin 56
  garlic mushroom & rosemary
    "vol au vents" 86
  Hawaiian pizza 60
  last of the summer veggie stew
    & dumplings 143
  mini puff pizzas 34
  New Year's Eve ham & Stilton
    canapés 85
  pesto 17
  pesto cheese twists or pinwheels 14
  roasted tomato & feta soup 104
  sausage cobbler 150
  sausage, tomato, & bean tarts 31

Serrano ham, mozzarella, & pesto tarts  32
summer veggie lasagna  137
sun-dried tomato pesto, sausage, & cauliflower bake  128
tomato, feta, & chive tart  59
tumbet savory crumble  140
tuna melt tarts  21
upside down fish pie  54
upside down spanakopita  74
warm caprese salad with roasted tomato vinaigrette  109
zucchini, asparagus & eggplant parmigiana  132
zucchini & ricotta phyllo tart  66
cherries
 cherry Bakewell tart  184
 chocolate & berry Valentine's heart tart  91
 pineapple & rum cake  156
 pineapple puffs  181
chicken
 chicken parm pie  65
 chicken pot pie  50
 chicken thigh risotto  126
 chicken tikka pies  42
 marmalade & blood orange chicken bake  149
 roast in the hole  144
chickpeas: chopped salad with smoked chili-fried chickpeas  110
chili non-carne casserole  125
fries
 fish & chips pie  77
 Mother's Day shrimp & pommes frites tarts  94
chocolate
 Christmas pudding brownie pie  201
 pear & chocolate tarts  192
chocolate hazelnut spread: chocolate & berry Valentine's heart tart  91
Christmas pie, leftover  80
Christmas pudding brownie pie  201
cinnamon puffs  15
citrus & pistachio frangipane tart  196
cobbler
 Aperol, apricot, & peach cobbler  173
 plum & pear cobbler tart  198
 sausage cobbler  150
coconut flakes: mango, rum, & coconut tarts  195
coffee: banana, coffee, & cinnamon cake  158
cornichons
 tartar sauce  17
 tuna melt tarts  21
Cornish pasties, upside down  44
cottage cheese
 fish & chips pie  77
 leftover veggie slaw with mint, pea, & cottage cheese dressing  112
cranberry sauce
 Halloween sausage & cranberry "mummy" heads  97

leftover Christmas pie  80
cream
 apple & honey bread & butter pudding  168
 hot & cold Eton mess tart  182
 salted caramel banana loaf  164
 spinach, pea, & sausage eggs Florentine  138
 veggie sausage, shallot, & bean tagliatelle bake  134
cream cheese
 banana, toffee, & cream cheese tarts  188
 cheesy potato tarts  25
 chilled leek, potato, & lemongrass soup  106
 chopped salad with smoked chili-fried chickpeas  110
 creamy mushroom oven-baked orzotto  131
 garlic mushroom & rosemary "vol au vents"  86
 shallot & cream cheese tarts  20
 smoked salmon & cream cheese canapés  98
 summer veggie lasagna  137
crumble, tumbet savory  140
cucumber
 chilled leek, potato, & lemongrass soup  106
 chopped salad with smoked chili-fried chickpeas  110
 fattoushanella salad  118

# D

dumplings: last of the summer veggie stew & dumplings  143

# E

eggplant
 zucchini, asparagus, & eggplant parmigiana  132
 tumbet savory crumble  140
eggs
 full English breakfast pie  53
 homemade mayonnaise  17
 spinach, pea, & sausage eggs Florentine  138
 tartar sauce  17
equipment  10–11
Eton mess tart, hot & cold  182

#

fattoushanella salad  118
fennel
 chilled leek, potato, & lemongrass soup  106
 chili non-carne casserole  125
 roasted potato, beef, & bean hot pot  146
fish
 Burns Night Cullen skink canapés  88
 fish & chips pie  77
 smoked salmon & cream cheese canapés  98
 tuna melt tarts  21
 upside down fish pie  54
French onion soup tarte tatin  56
fruit see also specific fruit
 fruit gelatin mold  167
 summer berry bread pudding  174
full English breakfast pie  53

# G

garlic mushroom & rosemary "vol au vents"  86
gelatin: fruit gelatin mold  167
ginger loaf cake, Grandma Jennie's  176
golden syrup: steamed syrup cake  170
Grandma Jennie's ginger loaf cake  176
green beans
 last of the summer veggie stew & dumplings  143
 sausage cobbler  150
 summer veggie lasagna  137
 warm caprese salad with roasted tomato vinaigrette  109

# H

Halloween sausage & cranberry "mummy" heads  97
ham
 asparagus & Ibérico ham tarts  28
 Hawaiian pizza  60
 New Year's Eve ham & Stilton canapés  85
 Serrano ham, mozzarella, & pesto tarts  32
hash browns: full English breakfast pie  53
Hawaiian pizza  60
herringbone rhubarb tart  190
honey  10
 Aperol, apricot, & peach cobbler  173
 apple & honey bread & butter pudding  168
 beet, red onion, & goat cheese tart  48
 chili shrimp, honey, & bacon canapés  82

203

chocolate & berry Valentine's heart tart 91
mango, rum, & coconut tarts 195
pineapple puffs 181
horseradish sauce: tuna melt tarts 21
hot & cold Eton mess tart 182

## I

ice cream: hot & cold Eton mess tart 182
ingredients 10–11

## J

jam
  apple & berry compote lattice pie 187
  cherry Bakewell tart 184
  hot & cold Eton mess tart 182

## K

kale: roasted potato & tomato salad 115
kugel: potato, carrot, & onion 103

## L

lasagna, summer veggie 137
last of the summer veggie stew & dumplings 143
leeks
  cheesy leek tart 62
  chilled leek, potato, & lemongrass soup 106
leftover Christmas pie 80
leftover veggie slaw with mint, pea, & cottage cheese dressing 112
lemongrass: chilled leek, potato, & lemongrass soup 106
lemons
  apricot, polenta, & almond cake 155
  Brussels sprout Caesar salad 121
  chopped salad with smoked chili-fried chickpeas 110
  citrus & pistachio frangipane tart 196
  fish & chips pie 77
  zucchini & ricotta phyllo tart 66
limes: mango, rum, & coconut tarts 195

## M

mango, rum, & coconut tarts 195
marmalade & blood orange chicken bake 149
marshmallows: chocolate & berry Valentine's heart tart 91
mayonnaise, homemade 17
meringues: hot & cold Eton mess tart 182
milk
  apple & honey bread & butter

pudding 168
chilled leek, potato, & lemongrass soup 106
summer veggie lasagna 137
upside down fish pie 54
white sauce 16
mint: leftover veggie slaw with mint, pea, & cottage cheese dressing 112
monkey pie crust 15
Mother's Day shrimp & pommes frites tarts 94
mushrooms
  chicken pot pie 50
  creamy mushroom oven-baked orzotto 131
  full English breakfast pie 53
  garlic mushroom & rosemary "vol au vents" 86
  last of the summer veggie stew & dumplings 143
  roast in the hole 144
  sun-dried tomato pesto, sausage, & cauliflower bake 128
mustard
  sausage, red onion, & mustard tarts 38
  St. Patrick's day bacon & colcannon pie 92

## N

nettles: cherry tomato, nettle, & mozzarella phyllo tart 68
New Year's Eve ham & Stilton canapés 85
nuts
  Aperol, apricot, & peach cobbler 173
  apricot, polenta, & almond cake 155
  blueberry & apple muffin cake 161
  cherry Bakewell tart 184
  citrus & pistachio frangipane tart 196
  pear & chocolate tarts 192
  plum & pear cobbler tart 198

## O

oats: blueberry & apple muffin cake 161
oils 10, 16
olive oil: blood orange olive oil cake 162
olives
  Halloween sausage & cranberry "mummy" heads 97
  spinach, pea, & sausage eggs Florentine 138
onions
  beet, red onion, & goat cheese tart 48
  chicken thigh risotto 126
  chili non-carne casserole 125
  feta, tomato, & strawberry panzanella salad 116
  French onion soup tarte tatin 56
  last of the summer veggie stew & dumplings 143

marmalade & blood orange chicken bake 149
mini puff pizzas 34
potato, carrot, & onion kugel 103
roast in the hole 144
roasted potato, beef, & bean hot pot 146
sausage, mashed potato, & gravy pie 71
sausage, red onion, & mustard tarts 38
Serrano ham, mozzarella, & pesto tarts 32
spinach, pea, & sausage eggs Florentine 138
upside down Cornish pasties 44
oranges
  blood orange olive oil cake 162
  citrus & pistachio frangipane tart 196
  marmalade & blood orange chicken bake 149

## P

pasta
  creamy mushroom oven-baked orzotto 131
  summer veggie lasagna 137
  veggie sausage, shallot, & bean tagliatelle bake 134
pastry
  cinnamon puffs 15
  classic pie dough 13
  monkey pie crust 15
  pesto cheese twists or pinwheels 14
  premade 10–11
  simple puff pastry 12
peaches: Aperol, apricot, & peach cobbler 173
pears
  pear & chocolate tarts 192
  plum & pear cobbler tart 198
peas
  Brussels sprout Caesar salad 121
  chicken pot pie 50
  chopped salad with smoked chili-fried chickpeas 110
  creamy mushroom oven-baked orzotto 131
  fish & chips pie 77
  last of the summer veggie stew & dumplings 143
  leftover veggie slaw with mint, pea, & cottage cheese dressing 112
  spinach, pea, & sausage eggs Florentine 138
  summer veggie lasagna 137
  upside down fish pie 54
  upside down vegetable samosas 37
pepperoni: mini puff pizzas 34
peppers
  Halloween sausage & cranberry "mummy" heads 97
  tumbet savory crumble 140
pesto
  homemade pesto 17

Serrano ham, mozzarella, & pesto tarts 32
sun-dried tomato pesto, sausage, & cauliflower bake 128
pesto cheese twists or pinwheels 14
pineapple
Hawaiian pizza 60
pineapple & rum cake 156
pineapple puffs 181
pine nuts
pesto 17
sun-dried tomato pesto, sausage, & cauliflower bake 128
pistachios: citrus & pistachio frangipane tart 196
pizza
Hawaiian pizza 60
mini puff pizzas 34
plant-based meat alternative: chili non-carne casserole 125
plum & pear cobbler tart 198
polenta: apricot, polenta, & almond cake 155
potatoes
Burns Night Cullen skink canapés 88
cheesy potato tarts 25
chilled leek, potato, & lemongrass soup 106
chili non-carne casserole 125
fish & chips pie 77
last of the summer veggie stew & dumplings 143
leftover Christmas pie 80
Mother's Day shrimp & pommes frites tarts 94
potato, carrot, & onion kugel 103
roast in the hole 144
roasted potato & tomato salad 115
roasted potato, beef, & bean hot pot 146
roasted tomato & feta soup 104
sausage cobbler 150
sausage, mashed potato, & gravy pie 71
St. Patrick's day bacon & colcannon pie 92
tumbet savory crumble 140
upside down Cornish pasties 44
upside down vegetable samosas 37

## R

radishes: fattoushanella salad 118
rhubarb: herringbone rhubarb tart 190
rice
burrito pie 72
chicken thigh risotto 126
ricotta: zucchini & ricotta phyllo tart 66
roast in the hole 144
rum
mango, rum, & coconut tarts 195
pineapple & rum cake 156
rutabaga: upside down Cornish pasties 44

## S

salads
Brussels sprout Caesar salad 121
chopped salad with smoked chili-fried chickpeas 110
fattoushanella salad 118
feta, tomato, & strawberry panzanella salad 116
leftover veggie slaw with mint, pea, & cottage cheese dressing 112
roasted potato & tomato salad 115
warm caprese salad with roasted tomato vinaigrette 109
samosas, upside down vegetable 37
sauces
cheesy sauce 54
slow-cooked tomato sauce 16
tartar sauce 17
white sauce 16
sausage
full English breakfast pie 53
Halloween sausage & cranberry "mummy" heads 97
leftover Christmas pie 80
roast in the hole 144
sausage cobbler 150
sausage, mashed potato, & gravy pie 71
sausage, red onion, & mustard tarts 38
sausage, tomato, & bean tarts 31
spinach, pea, & sausage eggs Florentine 138
sun-dried tomato pesto, sausage, & cauliflower bake 128
veggie sausage, shallot, & bean tagliatelle bake 134
sausage cobbler 150
seafood
Mother's Day shrimp & pommes frites tarts 94
sesame shrimp toast tarts 26
Serrano ham, mozzarella, & pesto tarts 32
sesame shrimp toast tarts 26
shallots
cherry tomato, nettle, & mozzarella phyllo tart 68
chicken pot pie 50
chilled leek, potato, & lemongrass soup 106
fattoushanella salad 118
French onion soup tarte tatin 56
roasted potato & tomato salad 115
sausage cobbler 150
shallot & cream cheese tarts 20
summer veggie lasagna 137
sun-dried tomato pesto, sausage, & cauliflower bake 128
veggie sausage, shallot, & bean tagliatelle bake 134
shrimp
chili shrimp, honey, & bacon canapés 82
Mother's Day shrimp & pommes frites tarts 94
sesame shrimp toast tarts 26

upside down fish pie 54
slaws: leftover veggie slaw with mint, pea, & cottage cheese dressing 112
smoked salmon & cream cheese canapés 98
soups
chilled leek, potato, & lemongrass soup 106
roasted tomato & feta soup 104
sour cream: chili non-carne casserole 125
spanakopita, upside down 74
spinach
spinach, pea, & sausage eggs Florentine 138
upside down spanakopita 74
veggie sausage, shallot, & bean tagliatelle bake 134
steamed syrup cake 170
St. Patrick's day bacon & colcannon pie 92
strawberries
chocolate & berry Valentine's heart tart 91
feta, tomato, & strawberry panzanella salad 116
hot & cold Eton mess tart 182
summer berry bread pudding 174

## T

tartar sauce 17
tarts, savory
asparagus & Ibérico ham tarts 28
beet, red onion, & goat cheese tart 48
burrito pie 72
carrot, cilantro, & feta tarts 41
cheesy leek tart 62
cheesy potato tarts 25
cherry tomato, nettle, & mozzarella phyllo tart 68
chicken parm pie 65
chicken pot pie 50
chicken tikka pies 42
fish & chips pie 77
French onion soup tarte tatin 56
full English breakfast pie 53
Halloween sausage & cranberry "mummy" heads 97
Hawaiian pizza 60
leftover Christmas pie 80
mini puff pizzas 34
Mother's Day shrimp & pommes frites tarts 94
sausage, mashed potato, & gravy pie 71
sausage, red onion, & mustard tarts 38
sausage, tomato, & bean tarts 31
Serrano ham, mozzarella, & pesto tarts 32
sesame shrimp toast tarts 26
shallot & cream cheese tarts 20
St. Patrick's day bacon & colcannon pie 92
tomato, feta, & chive tart 59

tuna melt tarts  21
upside down Cornish pasties  44
upside down fish pie  54
upside down spanakopita  74
upside down vegetable samosas  37
zucchini & ricotta phyllo tart  66
tarts, sweet
  apple & berry compote lattice pie  187
  banana, toffee, & cream cheese tarts  188
  cherry Bakewell tart  184
  chocolate & berry Valentine's heart tart  91
  citrus & pistachio frangipane tart  196
  herringbone rhubarb tart  190
  hot & cold Eton mess tart  182
  mango, rum, & coconut tarts  195
  pear & chocolate tarts  192
  pineapple puffs  181
  plum & pear cobbler tart  198
tomato chutney: chicken tikka pies  42
tomatoes
  cherry tomato, nettle, & mozzarella phyllo tart  68
  chili non-carne casserole  125
  chopped salad with smoked chili-fried chickpeas  110
  fattoushanella salad  118
  feta, tomato, & strawberry panzanella salad  116
  Halloween sausage & cranberry "mummy" heads  97
  roasted potato & tomato salad  115
  roasted tomato & feta soup  104
  slow-cooked tomato sauce  16

sun-dried tomato pesto, sausage, & cauliflower bake  128
tomato, feta, & chive tart  59
warm caprese salad with roasted tomato vinaigrette  109
tomato sauce
  chicken parm pie  65
  chili shrimp, honey & bacon canapés  82
  fish & chips pie  77
  Hawaiian pizza  60
  mini puff pizzas  34
  sausage, tomato, & bean tarts  31
  slow-cooked tomato sauce  16
  tumbet savory crumble  140
  zucchini, asparagus, & eggplant parmigiana  132
tumbet savory crumble  140
tuna melt tarts  21
turkey: leftover Christmas pie  80

## V

vegetables *see also* specific vegetables
  leftover Christmas pie  80
"vol au vents," garlic mushroom & rosemary  86

## W

white sauce  16

## Y

yogurt
  blood orange olive oil cake  162
  Brussels sprout Caesar salad  121
  chicken tikka pies  42
  chili non-carne casserole  125
  chopped salad with smoked chili-fried chickpeas  110
  roasted potato & tomato salad  115
Yorkshire pudding, roast in the hole  144

## Z

zucchini
  last of the summer veggie stew & dumplings  143
  summer veggie lasagna  137
  sun-dried tomato pesto, sausage, & cauliflower bake  128
  tumbet savory crumble  140
  zucchini, asparagus, & eggplant parmigiana  132
  zucchini & ricotta phyllo tart  66

# About the Author

**Dominic Franks** is a food writer and home cook who was takes inspiration from Delia Smith and his Mum, his Jewish heritage, and his London upbringing. He lives in Lincolnshire with his husband Andy where he has been cooking and writing his food blog *Dom in the Kitchen* since 2010. He writes for *Lincolnshire Life Magazine* and is regularly featured on *BBC Radio Lincolnshire* as their food expert.

You can find Dom's blog at **dominthekitchen.com** and his instagram is **@dominthekitchen**

# Acknowledgments

I have never written a book before and while I've always wanted to, I really had no idea what the process would entail. It's been a whirlwind experience but has also felt at times like things were going in slow-mo and I've just been staring slack-jawed into the middle distance with a smile on my face. However, importantly, I've had the most incredibly supportive people around me, who have guided me through every step of the way, both professionally and emotionally. I have a lot of people I'd like thank for this guidance.

I want to start by thanking my literary agent, Liza, who's girlish chuckle hides a whip-smart brain and fabulous capacity for Champagne consumption. She led me to the incredible team at DK Books, who have literally and figuratively held my hand through the process. Cara, Lucy, and Tania have been so lovely and Nicky, my editor, is like the English teacher I've always wanted but never got. Thank you all.

Thank you to Ellis Parrinder, Max Robinson, and Susannah Unsworth—my photographer, stylist, and food stylist—who literally crawled inside my brain and extracted my thoughts to create a unique vision for this book.

Thank you to Nikki at Nic & Lou, who just seemed to get me and managed to design the beautiful artwork and layout of the book based on a few simple questions about where I buy my shirts!

Thank you to Pauline at Nordic Ware for providing me with the most wonderful baking sheets, bundt pans, and cake tins. You and they really are the best!

Clearly, I would be nowhere without my mum. Thank you for the inspiration and always having a recipe tucked away somewhere that just seemed to work when I needed it. Thank you to my dad for always taking us to amazing restaurants when we were kids and probably way too young to truly appreciate them. I obviously did. And, of course, thank you to my whole family for believing I would eventually actually do something.

I'd like to thank Lisa for always dishing out the best f*** 'em advice, being my greatest cheerleader, never taking any bullshit, and for grounding me when my head gets too big. And to all my friends who have always been there, even if I don't call as often as I should.

Importantly, I want to thank all my social media followers who constantly pestered me for a cookbook—so much so that I actually started to believe that I should write one. I did promise you one and here it is!

And finally, I want to tell you about my incredible husband, Andy (The Viking), who is always my biggest champion, forever my safety net, and somehow able to talk me down off a cliff even though at times I seemed incapable of expressing emotions other than spitting venom, which he takes without complaint. I love you Andy and could not have done this without you. You are my everything.

### Publisher's Acknowledgments

DK would like to thank Sarah Epton for proofreading, Ruth Ellis for providing the index, and Renee Wilmeth for US consulting.

### DK LONDON

**Editorial Director** Cara Armstrong
**Senior Designer and Jacket Designer** Tania Gomes
**Senior Editor** Lucy Sienkowska
**Senior US Editor** Megan Douglass
**DTP and Design Coordinator** Heather Blagden
**Jacket and Sales Material Coordinator** Emily Cannings
**Senior Production Editor** Tony Phipps
**Senior Production Controller** Samantha Cross
**Art Director** Maxine Pedliham
**Publishing Director** Stephanie Jackson

**Editorial** Nicola Graimes
**Design** Amy Child
**Design Development and Illustrations** Studio Nic & Lou
**Photography** Ellis Parrinder
**Food Styling** Susanna Unsworth
**Prop Styling** Max Robinson

First American Edition, 2025
Published in the United States by DK Publishing,
a division of Penguin Random House LLC
1745 Broadway, 20th Floor New York, NY 10019

Text Copyright © Dominic Franks 2025
Dominic Franks has asserted his right to be identified as the
author of this work.
Copyright © 2025 Dorling Kindersley Limited
25 26 27 28 29 10 9 8 7 6 5 4 3 2 1
001–348666–Jun/2025

All rights reserved.
Without limiting the rights under the copyright reserved above,
no part of this publication may be reproduced, stored in or
introduced into a retrieval system, or transmitted, in any form, or
by any means (electronic, mechanical, photocopying, recording,
or otherwise), without the prior written permission of the
copyright owner.
Published in Great Britain by Dorling Kindersley Limited

ISBN: 978-0-5939-6912-0

Printed and bound in China

**www.dk.com**

This book was made with Forest Stewardship Council™ certified paper—one small step in DK's commitment to a sustainable future. Learn more at www.dk.com/uk/information/sustainability